Eat Smart in Peru

Eat Smart in Peru

How to Decipher the Menu
Know the Market Foods
&
Embark on a Tasting Adventure

Joan Peterson and Brook Soltvedt

Illustrated by Susan Chwae

GINKGO PRESS™ INC

Madison, Wisconsin

Eat Smart in Peru
Joan B. Peterson and Brook C. Soltvedt

Although the author and publisher have exhaustively researched all sources to ensure the accuracy and completeness of the information contained in this book, we assume no responsibility for errors, inaccuracies, omissions or any inconsistency herein. Any slights of people or organizations are unintentional.

Map lettering is by Gail L. Carlson; cover and insert photographs are by Joan Peterson; author photographs are by Susan Chwae.

The quote by James A. Michener from "This Great Big Wonderful World," from the March 1956 issue of Travel-Holiday Magazine, © 1956 by James A. Michener, is reprinted by permission of William Morris Agency, LLC on behalf of the author.

Publisher's Cataloging-in-Publication
(Provided by Quality Books, Inc.)
Peterson, Joan (Joan B.)
   Eat smart in Peru : how to decipher the menu, know
the market foods & embark on a tasting adventure / Joan
Peterson and Brook Soltvedt ; illustrated by Susan
Chwae.
   p. cm.
   Includes bibliographical references and index.
   LCCN 2005936692
   ISBN-13: 978-0-9641168-0-1
   ISBN-10: 0-9641168-0-4

   1. Cookery, Peruvian. 2. Food habits--Peru. 3. Peru
--Guidebooks.   I. Soltvedt, Brook Chase, 1959-
II. Title.

TX716.P4P48 2006   641.5985
             QBI05-600183

Printed in the United States of America

To Debora Jacobs

Her love and knowledge of Peruvian food
added savor to every page.

Contents

Resources   73

A listing of stores carrying hard-to-find Peruvian foods and groups offering opportunities for person-to-person contact through home visits to gain a deeper understanding of the country, including its cuisine.

Helpful Phrases   77

Phrases in English transliterated to Spanish, with additional phonetic interpretation, which will assist you in finding, ordering and buying foods or ingredients.

Menu Guide   81

An extensive listing of menu entries in Spanish (with some Quechua), with English translations, to make ordering food an easy and immediately rewarding experience.

Foods and Flavors Guide   109

A comprehensive glossary of ingredients, kitchen utensils and cooking methods in Spanish (with some Quechua), with English translations.

Restaurants   137

Chefs at these eateries taught us much about Peruvian Food.

Preface

If you reject the food, ignore the customs, fear the religion and avoid the people, you might better stay home. You are like a pebble thrown into water; you become wet on the surface but you are never a part of the water.

— JAMES A. MICHENER

There is no more satisfying way to get immersed in a new culture than to mingle with local people in the places where they enjoy good food and conversation—in their favorite neighborhood cafés, restaurants, picnic spots or outdoor markets. We try to capture the essence of a country through its food, and seek out unfamiliar ingredients and preparations that provide new tastes. By meandering on foot or navigating on local buses, we have discovered serendipitously many memorable eateries away from more heavily trafficked tourist areas.

The purpose of the EAT SMART guides is to encourage sampling new and often unusual foods, and to discover new ways of preparing or combining familiar ingredients. What better way is there to get to know a culture than through its cuisine? We know informed travelers will be more open to experimentation. The EAT SMART guides also will help steer the traveler away from foods they want to avoid—everyone confesses to disliking something!

This guide has four main chapters. The first provides a history of Peruvian cuisine. It is followed by a chapter with descriptions of regional Peruvian foods. The other main chapters are extensive listings, placed near the end of the book for easy reference. The *Menu Guide* is an alphabetical compilation of menu entries, including general Peruvian fare as well as regional specialties.

Some not-to-be-missed dishes with country-wide popularity are labeled "national favorite" in the margin next to the menu entry. Some classic regional dishes of Peru—also not to be missed—are labeled "regional classic." The *Foods & Flavors Guide* contains a translation of food items and terms associated with preparing and serving food. This glossary will be useful in interpreting menus, since it is impractical to cover in the *Menu Guide* all the flavors or combinations possible for certain dishes.

Also included in the book is a chapter offering hints on browsing and shopping in the food markets and one with phrases that will be useful in restaurants and food markets to learn more about the foods of Peru. A chapter is devoted to classic and *novoandino* Peruvian recipes. Do take time to experiment with these recipes before departure; it is a wonderful and immediately rewarding way to preview Peruvian food. Most special Peruvian ingredients in these recipes can be obtained in the United States; substitutions for unavailable ingredients are given. Sources of hard-to-find Peruvian ingredients can be found in the *Resources* chapter, which also cites groups that offer the opportunity to have person-to-person contact through home visits to gain a deeper understanding of the country, including its cuisine.

JOAN PETERSON & BROOK SOLTVEDT
Madison, Wisconsin

Acknowledgments

We gratefully acknowledge those who assisted us in preparing this book. Thanks to Susan Chwae (Ginkgo Press) for illustrations, cover design and author photographs; Gail Carlson for enlivening our maps with her handwriting; and Nicol Knappen (Ekeby) for book design.

For contributing recipes (regrettably, some could not be used because of space limitations) and/or providing cooking demonstrations we thank Marita Landaveri (Consul General of Peru, Denver, Colorado); executive chef Adolfo M. Perret Bermúdez and Gabriela Fiorini de Perret (co-owners, Punta Sal Restaurants, Lima); Luis Felipe Arizola Gadea (executive chef/owner, A Puerta Cerrada Restaurant, Lima); Liliana Com (general manager, Wa Lok Restaurant, Lima); Jorge (Coque) Luis Ossio Guiulfo (executive chef/owner, La Bombonniere, Lima, and the Inka Grill, Cuzco); Marisa Guiulfo Zender (founder, Guiulfo catering and restaurant empire, Lima); Rafael Piqueras (executive chef, Sonesta Posadas del Inca, Lima); Roxanna Freundt de Salaverry and Alberto Salaverry (owners, Manos Morenos Restaurant, Lima); Flavio Solórzano Alvarez (executive chef, El Señorío de Sulco, Lima); Marilú Madueño (chef, Restaurant Huaca Pucllana, Lima); Ana Debert de Kesch (chef/owner, Club Colonial Restaurant, Huanchaco, Trujillo); Hernan Castañeda (chef, Map Café, Cuzco); Santiago Solari Morgan (chef/owner, Ñaylamp Restaurant, Lima); Michael Raas (corporate executive chef, Orient-Express Peruvian Hotels, Cuzco); Eduardo Pasquel and Juan José Mendoza (food and beverage manager and general manager, respectively, Sonesta Posadas del Inca, Yucay); Denise Koechlin, co-owner, and José Luis Massa, food and beverage manager (Machu Picchu Pueblo Hotel and InkaTerra Café, Machu Picchu Pueblo Village); Teresa Bancallán de Castillo and Lizandro Castillo Salazar (co-owners, El Rincón del Pato Restaurant, Lambayeque); Fidel Trigozo (chef/owner, El

Tiradito, Lima); Guillermo de la Fuente Sattui (chef, Hotel Paracas, Paracas); Gloria Yaipén Chafloque, chef, and César Flores Yaipén, owner (La Perla de las Flores Restaurant, Chiclayo); Alcario Callyahua, chef, and Celmira Cerpa, owner (Sol de Mayo Restaurant, Arequipa); Alberto Solis Serrepe (owner, Fiesta Restaurante Gourmet, Lambayeque); Cristel Carrasco Gonzales (owner, El Catador Restaurant and Winery, Ica); Diego Garcia Vela, (chef, El Dorado Plaza Hotel, Iquitos); M.J. Vazquez family (Hacienda Paiján, Paiján); Ines and Antonio Caycho (owners, El Huerto de mi Amada, Azpitia, Lima); Maria de Lam (chef/owner, Huanchaco Beach Restaurant, Trujillo); Teresa Cilloniz, owner, and Celinda Reyes Farfán, food manager (Casa-Hacienda San José, Chincha); Cucho La Rosa (director, Cenfotur culinary program, Lima); Felipe Antonio Custer (executive president, Corporación Custer, Lima); Antonio Cossio Arana (chef/owner, Tunupa Restaurant, Cuzco and Sacred Valley); and Javier and Jodie Castañeda (United States).

We are indebted to many people for introducing us to regional foods, for help in identifying regional Peruvian foods and menu items, for reading the manuscript, for providing resource materials, or for guide and tourist services. Thanks to Eloy Alfaro (Embassy of Peru, Washington, DC); Maria Isabel Leon de Cespedes (Iberoamericana de Hotelería y Turismo, Lima); Víctor A. Ruiz Bernales (Fabrica de Chocolates y Tejas Helena, Ica); La Iberica Chocolate Factory (Arequipa); Astrid Dr. Oswaldo Henrique Urbano (Instituto de Investigación, Universidad de San Martín de Turismo y Hotelería, Lima); Dr. William Roca and Dr. Merideth Bonierbale (International Potato Center—CIP, Lima); Felipe Antonio Custer (Corporación Custer, Lima); Bernardo Roca Rey Miró Quesada (El Comercio Media, Lima); Dr. Fernando Cabieses (Universidad Científica del Sur); Walter W. Wust (food writer/photographer, Lima); Javier and Jodie Castañeda, Berta Armaquanqui, Ted Ballweg, Alfonso Gutierrez and Javier Arana (United States); and tourist guides Rosario Talavera (Arequipa), Rolf Roeting and Alejandra Cabieses (Lima); Rosa Núñez (Cuzco); Ana Hueda (Trujillo), Alberto Flores (Chiclayo), Daniel Rios (Iquitos), and Susie and Julie Takash (Tarapoto and United States).

We gratefully acknowledge the expert assistance of Debora Jacobs (owner, Peru Options, Lima) for an itinerary that filled our needs perfectly, and for the background information she always found time to provide while we were writing this guide.

Guyana
Venezuela
Surinam
French Guiana
Colombia
Ecuador
Peru
Brazil
Bolivia
Chile
Paraguay
Argentina
Uruguay

South America

The Cuisine of Peru

An Historical Survey

The Republic of Peru, situated on the western coast of South America between Ecuador and Chile, is divided longitudinally into three topographical zones—the *costa* (coast), the *sierra* (mountains) and the *selva* (jungle). The zones possess remarkably distinct environments and cultural diversity, and each zone itself is characterized by astonishing environmental heterogeneity. Offshore, the plankton-rich cold Humboldt current supports a huge fish population, providing a significant maritime region under Peruvian sovereignty.

The *costa* is bordered on the west by the Pacific Ocean and on the east by the Andes. It comprises a narrow, snaking, bleak strip of sandy desert, sometimes rocky, often with rolling sand dunes, and extends into the foothills of the Andes. The zone receives scant rainfall as mist. Relatively little moisture evaporates from the cold waters of the Humboldt current running along the coast, and the hot desert air holds that moisture as it blows east up the slopes of the Andes. Clouds that form rarely release any rain until they are over the mountains. The Peruvian coastal region varies in width from about 50 to 100 miles and rises from sea level to about 6500 feet. It is almost uninhabitable except where fertile river valley oases cut across it from east to west. Fifty or more rivers arise in the Andes and flow down its western slopes. About 40 of these have sufficient volume to irrigate the valleys and create highly productive agricultural areas. Peru's major cities and economic centers are located in the coastal zone. More than a third of the population of Peru lives in Lima, the nation's capital, which is located in the Rímac Valley, about halfway down Peru's coast.

The *sierra* zone, the high central portion of Peru, includes the mountains, glaciers, plateaus, highland valleys, deep gorges, lakes and rivers of the Andes. It varies in width from about 150 miles in the north to about 250 miles in the south. The mountains rise from about 6500 feet above sea level

1

to the highest peak, Huascarán, at 22,199 feet. Between altitudes of 12,800 to 16,500 feet is the *puna,* or high Andean plateau, a cold, extremely harsh environment with rarified air. This almost treeless, windswept region is the highest area suitable for human habitation. Its year-round rivers, flat lakeshore plains and rolling grasslands characterized by clumps of native bunch grasses called *ichu* by the local people, provide ideal pasture for herds of camelids (llama, alpaca and vicuña). Agriculture is severely limited at the higher *puna* altitudes. In southern Peru, the *puna* widens extensively into what is called the *altiplano,* with Lake Titicaca, the world's highest navigable lake, at its southern tip. At a lower altitude, between 6500 and 11,500 feet, are the *kichwa,* or fertile highland valleys, with a wide range of ecological niches. The *kichwa* have served as one of the world's principal areas for plant domestication.

The largest zone of Peru—twice as large as the rest of the country—is the vast *selva* in eastern Peru. It begins at about 11,000 feet as a dense cloud forest shrouded in mist and fog, high up on the eastern slopes of the Andes, and continues down to about 300 feet. Copious rainfall makes possible a lush environment of extraordinary biodiversity. This part of the *selva* is known as the *ceja de selva* (brow of the jungle) or *montaña.* The lowland tropical jungle is relatively flat and essentially inaccessible by land. It surrounds the wide and winding Amazon river, which has its origin in glacier-fed rivers in the Andes. The small amount of arable land present in this scarcely populated zone occurs largely along the river banks. Most cities and villages are on the banks of the larger rivers.

Early History through Pre-Inca Civilizations

Human habitation in Peru began sometime before 9000 BCE. Early peoples were hunters and gatherers, occupying a number of coastal valleys in northern and central Peru, as well as the highland valley and *puna* regions of the Andes.

Archeologists study middens, or refuse piles, found at settlements to reveal the diet of primitive pre-ceramic cultures. The presence of mixtures of wild and cultivated plants indicates a transition to agriculture. Radiocarbon dating of shells, bones and carbonized seeds can place a civilization in time. Such studies provide evidence of plant cultivation by about 8000 BCE and sedentary village life by about 6000 BCE. Ceramics were not present until about 1800 BCE.

Analyses of middens show that the diet of early coastal cultures included marine shellfish, fish, chile peppers, squash, sweet potatoes, various tubers, beans, gourds, *pacae* (a huge, boomerang-shaped legume), guava and *lúcuma,* a green-skinned fruit still especially prized today. In the highlands, beans, squash, fruits, chile peppers, gourds, potatoes and other tubers, deer, camelids (llama, alpaca and vicuña) and guinea pig were eaten. In both geographical areas, cotton was cultivated. Trading between the highland and coastal groups was already taking place prior to the second millennium BCE as evidenced by the presence of non-native foods in the deposits: marine fish and shellfish in some highland middens and indigenous highland tubers in some coastal middens. Some pre-ceramic period coastal and highland sites show evidence of experimentation with channeling river water into canals for irrigation, and in the highlands there were attempts at terrace agriculture to create arable land.

Early human occupation in the *puna* is exemplified by the findings at Pachamachay cave, located 14,000 feet above sea level near Lake Junín in the Junín department of Peru. Radiocarbon dating shows that humans occupied this cave for several millennia, from about 7000 BCE to 1500 BCE. The primitive societies transitioned from hunters of camelids, primarily vicuña, to herders of these animals, whose natural habitat was the *puna.* Because of the severe limitations on agriculture at this altitude, these people foraged for small grains (quinoa and amaranth), starchy tubers, legumes and a high-altitude variety of prickly pear cactus.

The rugged eastern slope of the Andes and the lowland tropical jungle are less-well explored archaeologically. Crops domesticated in the *selva,* such as peanuts, sweet potatoes, yuca and coca, clearly had an impact on agriculture in the other zones, and their presence in these other zones provides evidence of the continuous trade and contact among these early cultures.

The huge pod of *pacae,* the ice cream bean, contains large seeds surrounded by sweet white pulp that is eaten fresh as a prized fruit snack. The pods of this legume can be up to 2 feet long and often are boomerang-shaped.

The archaeological record indicates that corn played a relatively minor role in the diet until about 1000 BCE. Early domesticated corn had tiny cobs with hard kernels and a sweet stalk. The theory that corn was initially domesticated and dispersed for the sugary pith of its stalks rather than as a cereal crop is a topic being studied vigorously today. Corn beer (*chicha*) made from fermented sugary stalk juice may well have been one of the first uses of corn by primitive cultures. Alcoholic beverages such as *chicha* were commonly consumed during rituals at ceremonial sites. Not until corn developed elongated cobs with many rows of large, soft kernels—the result of a long process of selection—did it become the prominent staple of most of the advanced cultures of Peru, and the sprouted kernels (*jora*) themselves become the prime starting material for making beer (*chicha de jora*).

By the time pottery production began around 1800 BCE, larger and more complex societies had developed. Agriculture had expanded in scale, and there was a shift toward increased plant domestication and centralized control of irrigation. Yet the inhabitants of these major population centers left no record of their societies because they had no written language. Recent archeological evidence indicates that some of these early civilizations used a sophisticated recording device called a *quipu* to convey information. The *quipu* is a series of knotted cords suspended vertically like a fringe from a stouter, horizontally held main cord. The device apparently carried financial and cultural information, although this information has yet to be deciphered. Until recently, the *quipu* had been thought to be an innovation of the Inca culture, which existed thousands of years later than these early cultures.

One of the best insights into ordinary family life is derived from abundant unearthed pottery artifacts belonging to the Moche civilization, which flourished between years the 100 and 750 along the banks of a dozen rivers between the Piura and Nepeña valleys on the northern coast. This civilization is probably the most famous pre-colonial South American culture because of the sculptural realism and narrative drawing of its finely modeled clay art. The remarkably expressive pottery vessels of the Moche cataloged daily life in rich detail. Painted pots, hand built or molded, many of which were stirrup-spout vessels, include houses, rafts, portraits of people and (not surprisingly) foods that were important to them. The lima bean, peanut, pepper, squash, corn, potato, sweet potato, avocado, *lúcuma* and *pepino dulce,* a striped fruit with refreshing, watery flesh, were common motifs, as were those of fowl, fish, shellfish, crabs, frogs, guinea pigs and game.

Elaborate drawings on Moche pottery show ceremonial rituals with people partaking of coca, a plant grown on the slopes of inland valleys and obtained by the Moche in trade from inhabitants in the *selva*. Scenes depicting corn beer (*chicha de jora*) preparation and consumption indicate that this beverage was also an important offering in Moche society rituals.

Basic village dwellings had three functional spaces: a large central area for living and sleeping, a primitive kitchen for food preparation and cooking, and a small space for large storage vessels. Within the kitchen were pens for guinea pigs to fatten up on food scraps before they were put into the stew pot themselves. The practice of raising guinea pigs in the kitchen for future consumption remains common in Peru today.

Occupational specialization in the Moche culture led to the formation of residential communities performing the same tasks. Communities of fishermen lived in small villages at the mouths of rivers and exchanged their maritime commodities for foods grown by agriculturalists living farther inland in the river valleys. An ambitious irrigation system linked several of the valleys. Goods were conveyed overland by llamas, pack animals traded from inhabitants of the Andes and bred by the Moche. Rafts built of *totora* reeds and balsa logs were used to haul nitrogen-rich bird guano from offshore islands in the Pacific to fertilize cultivated fields.

The Tiwanaku (Tiahuanaco) people contributed new patterns in food, drink and domestic routine that survived through subsequent periods in Peruvian history to modern times. Originating in the *altiplano* south of Lake Titicaca, now part of Bolivia, and expanding into the Moquegua Valley in southern Peru, this civilization existed between the years 450 and 1000. The Tiwanaku made non-ritual, social imbibing of alcoholic beverages (*chicha*) acceptable and promoted feasting that revolved around *chicha* consumption. They colonized corn-growing regions and introduced new, function-specific, impermeable pottery types for *chicha* production and

Moche-culture stirrup-spout vessel. The base depicts a cluster of sweet cucumber melons (*pepinos dulces*), which are still enjoyed today for their watery flesh.

consumption at feasts: flared drinking goblets, one-handled serving pitchers, flared bowls, and narrow-necked containers for storage, fermentation and transport of liquid. In the Moquegua Valley excavations of Tiwanaku villages reveal specialized community complexes representing primitive *chicherías* equipped to produce *chicha* on a large scale.

The huge and powerful Chimú empire was the largest civilization prior to the Inca. By the time it fell to the conquering Inca in 1470, it had spread out as far north as Tumbes at the border of present-day Ecuador and almost to present-day Lima in the south, covering a stretch of about 800 miles of the Pacific coast. In the tenth century, construction of the Chimú capital, Chan Chan, began in the Moche Valley. It ultimately occupied an area of about 12 square miles and became the great urban metropolis of the intervalley Chimú state.

Chan Chan comprised three categories of building complexes. There were 10 monumental royal compounds with labyrinthine inner sections, each compound including a palace and the state headquarters, and each enclosed by massive adobe walls over 30 feet high and 3 to 16 feet thick. When a ruler died, he was entombed in his palace, and another monumental compound was constructed for the subsequent ruler and his retinue. More than 30 intermediate complexes with low walls existed for nobility, and a great many smaller quarters served as dwellings for the commoners.

Agriculture was an important part of statecraft for the Chimú, the architects of the most extensive and complex canals ever built in the Moche Valley. Massive irrigation networks watered huge expanses of fields. Rural populations lived in planned hinterland communities. Simple buildings were established adjacent to large irrigated areas to house laborers working the fields. They primarily cultivated beans, squash, corn, avocados, *lúcuma,* chile peppers, cotton and gourds. In some instances, boggy areas were reclaimed by the use of raised fields, where corn and root crops were grown. Near the shore, sunken gardens were created by digging trenches down to the water table until sufficient moisture to sustain agriculture was reached. Such gardens fed the inhabitants of Chan Chan. Crop production and redistribution was controlled by the Chimú state administration.

The Inca

The Inca Empire developed from a small tribe of uncertain origin that settled in the region of Cuzco around 1200. The great Inca conquests began around 1438 with their victory over the Chanca tribe in Ayacucho. Around 1470 the Inca dismantled their most powerful rival, the Chimú, after a protracted struggle. This feat was ultimately achieved by sabotaging the Chimú's specialized irrigation system—their life blood. The Inca succeeded in their conquests in great part because of their ability to move men over an expansive, sophisticated network of stone roads they had built throughout the empire. By the time the Inca were vanquished by the Spanish in 1532, they had experienced explosive territorial expansion and extended their hegemony beyond modern Peru to parts of Ecuador, Chile, Bolivia and Argentina. In their endeavors, the Inca benefited from their cultural predecessors, whose knowledge they assimilated in forming an empire.

The Inca economy was a moneyless system based on agriculture. The state appropriated much of the empire's food and other commodities, which they stored in warehouses consisting of rows of large connected buildings. The state also controlled the subsequent redistribution of these goods. The availability of stores of state-owned food across the empire allowed Inca armies to travel swiftly, unburdened by the need to carry provisions on their backs. The Inca lacked a writing system, although crop yields and storage capacities were recorded using the system of knotted cords known as *quipus*. Cords of different colors and lengths had knots at different positions that appear to represent a decimal system.

Creating enough arable land to feed over five million mouths was an enormous challenge in the Inca empire, where much of the terrain was arid, densely forested or mountainous. To make up for the scarcity of flat agricultural land in the Andes, entire mountainsides were terraced and irrigated. Fertile soil, sand and pebbles for drainage, and large stones for building huge retaining walls all had to be hauled up the mountains. The Inca had a well-organized government and system of engineers to plan, coordinate and execute these projects to feed their people.

The accomplished Inca farmers apparently experimented with growing conditions at different altitudes. They knew that certain topographic configurations produced milder microclimates than the average climate typical of a particular area. On a limestone plateau about 24 miles from Cuzco, at an altitude of about 11,500 feet, are the remains of what appears to be a terraced agricultural research site, Moray. It is an awesome indication of the Inca's agricultural prowess. Using enormous natural cavities or depressions in the ground, Inca farmers sculpted six or seven concentric terraces within a cavity. The major cavity is only about 100 feet from the top to the bottom levels, yet the difference in average annual temperature between the top and bottom is about 59°F. Because each terrace is sheltered from the sun and wind to different degrees, a single multi-terraced depression at Moray replicates many different ecological zones of the Inca Empire. These terraces allowed Inca agriculturalists to test the ability of food crops to grow at different altitudes within their empire.

Much of what is known of Inca foodways derives from Spanish chroniclers. Corn was the most important commodity and dietary staple. It was cooked in many ways. Dried corn boiled in water made *muti,* which was the basic sustenance of the peasants. Flour made from ground dried corn was used to make dumplings called *humintas,* which were added to stew-like dishes. Ground fresh corn kernels were wrapped in cornhusks and boiled, a preparation also called *humintas (humitas).* Only women made corn beer (*chicha*), and the most common procedure was to use a chewed quid of corn (enzymes in human saliva) to start the fermentation process. *Chicha* was also made from other plants: quinoa, yuca, oca, carob and the pink pepper-like berry called *molle* from the Peruvian pepper tree (*Schinus molle*).

Potatoes were also a vital foodstuff of the Inca, who made a special feast dish, *pachamanca,* which required much preparation. It was a mixture of meats, potatoes and vegetables cooked over extremely hot volcanic stones in a covered pit in the ground. Another important ancient dish was *carapulcra (carapulca),* a stew made with dried potatoes (*papa seca*), flavored with peanuts and chile peppers. Both preparations are on the menu today.

In the Andean highlands, then and now, potatoes that were not eaten soon after harvest were preserved by a process of freeze-drying, and could be stored for several years without spoiling. The product, called *chuño*

Inca record keeper holding a knotted-string counting device (*quipu*). This is one of 400 drawings by the indigenous Felipe Guaman Poma de Ayala in his manuscript *The First New Chronicle and Good Government.* Finished in 1615, the book recounts Andean history.

blanco, or white *chuño,* is a lightweight, skinless nugget with characteristic hardness and chalky white color. White *chuño* is made with large, newly harvested, good-quality potatoes—any of several specific varieties of bitter potato. The potatoes are exposed to freezing nighttime temperatures and covered with straw during the day to prevent sun exposure and elevated daytime temperatures. After four days of freeze-thaw cycles, they are submerged for about a month in the icy waters of Andean streams to remove their bitterness. The potatoes are again frozen, but only overnight. On the following day they are stomped on with bare feet to remove most of the skin and press out much of the water content. The potatoes are further dehydrated by exposure to the sun for 10 to 15 days. *Chuño* can be ground into flour or softened in water for use in cooking.

Oca, olluco (melloco, ulluco), sweet potato and yuca were other tubers prominent in the Inca diet, but of secondary importance to potatoes. *Oca* and *olluco* are native to the highlands. *Oca* has brightly colored (white, yellow, pink, red, purple, or black) shiny tubers and crisp white flesh ranging in taste from sweet to tangy, depending on the variety. They were eaten raw, roasted or boiled. *Olluco* has colorful (white, pale-green, yellow, orange, pink or purple) tubers with crispy yellow flesh. The Inca appreciated the *olluco* tubers for their perceived medicinal properties.

Other foods important to the Inca included quinoa, a small nutritious grain, which was cooked like rice; beans, including the protein-rich *tarwi* (*chocho*), which were soaked in oil and eaten raw, stewed or boiled; and chile peppers, which were made into salsas to make other foods more palatable. A strong-flavored herb in the marigold family, *huacatay,* was an important seasoning, used fresh. Meat was more the province of the elite, who enjoyed camelids, Muscovy duck, guinea pig, deer, rabbit, partridge and water fowl. A kind of jerky (*charqui*) was made by drying camelid meat, primarily from llama and alpaca. The Inca made a fish preparation that is a precursor to today's *ceviche,* using the acidic, tart juice of the *tumbo,* a type of passion fruit, to "cook" the fish. After the Spanish conquistadors brought lemons and limes to Peru, *ceviches* were made with citrus juices.

Food from the sea was brought to the Andean highlands by a system of relay runners. The varieties included limpets, mussels, skates, rays, small sharks, and fish such as snook, mullet, bonito and sea catfish.

Saline springs in the highland valley northwest of Maras, near the terraced depressions of Moray, provided salt, harvested by the Inca much as it is today. The salt-saturated water flows out of the mountainside and is collected in several thousand small, contiguous pools constructed on the slope of the mountain. The salt solidifies when the water evaporates, and is broken down into crystals for sale in markets.

Inca kitchen hearths consisted of a small clay oven with round holes on top for pots and a small hole on one side for stirring the fire. Ceramic cookware in the homes of commoners included simple utilitarian pots and casseroles for cooking, jugs for making *chicha,* cups and glasses for drinking *chicha* and plates for serving. The imperial ceramic collection, by contrast, had a preponderance of highly decorated dinnerware.

The Spaniards

The military expansion and political success of the Inca Empire lasted less than a century. In 1532, motivated by tales of a wealthy native kingdom and its fabled hoards of gold to the south of Panama, the Spanish soldier and adventurer Francisco Pizarro and a small force of 106 foot soldiers and 62 horsemen landed in Tumbes on the northern coast of Peru. They arrived when the Inca Empire was at its zenith but caught up in a dynastic struggle between the presumed heir to the Inca throne, Huáscar, and his rival half brother, Atahualpa. This rift within the empire played into the hands of the Spaniards, who ultimately used subterfuge and their more powerful weapons to annihilate the Inca Empire. Spanish guns, swords and horses terrified the indigenous people, who had never seen such power. Despite their much smaller numbers, the Spanish easily conquered the empire.

Pizarro's forces met up with Atahualpa, the victorious of the rival Inca brothers, in the city of Cajamarca in the Andes. A battle ensued, during which thousands of Inca were slaughtered. Atahualpa himself was drawn into an ambush and held captive, leaving Pizarro effectively in control of the Inca Empire. The Spaniards exacted an enormous ransom for Atahualpa's freedom—a roomful of gold and two of silver. But in the end, the Spanish reneged on their pledge. Suspicious that Atahualpa had secretly sent for his generals to attack them, the Spaniards executed the Inca in 1533, nearly a year after taking him hostage. Pizarro marched on to Cuzco and installed a member of the Inca royal family as head of a puppet government to maintain the fiction of Inca rule. Although scattered rebellions against the Spanish continued until 1572, a colonial government was successfully established with its capital on the coast at Lima, the city founded by Pizarro in 1535, to make communication with Spain more reliable. The Viceroyalty of Peru was established in 1543 and Lima became the political, economic and cultural hub of Spanish colonial life in Peru.

The *encomienda* system was central to the economic and social organization of colonial Peru. It was a trusteeship adopted in 1503 by the Spanish Crown and used during the Spanish colonization of the Americas. The conquerors, known as *encomenderos* under this system, were to extract tribute for the Crown. In exchange, they were assigned rights to certain lands, giving them control over the labor and produce of the indigenous people living there. In the process, the Indians were to receive protection and be converted to Christianity. Not surprisingly, the *encomenderos* ruthlessly abused the system by appropriating additional land from the Indians, exacting increased taxes and forcing the natives into slavery. The *encomederos* widened their sphere of influence beyond agricultural pursuits and dominated the lucrative silver, gold and copper mining operations as well.

The Spanish added a multitude of new foodstuffs to the Peruvian kitchen, dramatically changing the dietary habits of the country. Creole (*criollo*) cuisine evolved from the fusion of Old and New World culinary traditions. Several Old World animals accompanied the Spanish on early voyages: pigs, cattle, sheep, goats, horses, burros and chickens. These animals not only provided new meat sources, but also introduced eggs and a variety of dairy products: cream, milk, cheese and butter. The Spanish brought new grains—wheat, rice and barley—and introduced a great many fruits and vegetables including onions, garlic, chickpeas, lentils, carrots, cabbage, lettuce, radishes, turnips, spinach, olives, peaches, pears, melons, apples, pears, pomegranates, grapes, citrus fruits, bananas and sugar cane, as well as olive oil, vinegar and wine.

Large plantations were established to grow crops for local consumption and export to Europe. Sugar cane, rice, olives and bananas were cultivated in the irrigated coastal valleys. Wheat prospered in the highland valleys; grapes grew in the southern coastal area. Cattle ranches were created in the lower valleys of the central Andes to provide meat and hides, as well as tallow for candles. Coca farms

Huacatay, a pungent herb with dark-green, jagged-edged leaves, which is used fresh as a seasoning. English names include black mint and Peruvian black marigold.

11

produced coca leaves for the workers in the gold and silver mines. The stimulant released when workers chewed the coca leaves increased their physical stamina and suppressed their appetites, making the extremely arduous work more tolerable.

Pre-colonial dishes were altered and enriched by the addition of Old World ingredients, and many are on today's menus. For example, milk, cheese, onion and garlic were added to *locro,* an ancient casserole-like dish of squash, potatoes, corn and chile peppers. Pork replaced guinea pig and onions and garlic were added to *carapulcra,* a stew of dried potatoes (*papa seca*) flavored with peanuts and chile peppers.

Popular colonial main dishes mixing New and Old World foodstuffs were *puchero,* a one-dish meal made by cooking beef, pork and mutton, especially lamb head, together with cabbage, sweet potatoes, blood sausage, pigs' feet, yuca, corn, banana, quince and chickpeas until mushy; and *chupe,* a chowder made with potatoes, shrimp, fish, eggs and cheese. Corn mixtures for tamales contained bits of meat, hard-boiled eggs and raisins.

A delicious dessert tradition is attributed to Catholic nuns, who established many convents in Lima. They had the monopoly on sweets before confectioners arrived in Peru. Continuing a tradition inherited from Moorish Spain, the nuns made rich sweet desserts using copious amounts of eggs and Peruvian sugar. Among the sweets they made were *chumpús de agrio y de leche,* a creamy mixture of milk and lemon juice; an *empanada* made with marzipan pastry; *alfajores,* sandwich cookies with a sweet milk caramel (*manjar blanco*) filling; and *ponderaciones,* crispy, deep-fried pastry swirls made with a spiral-shaped metal iron called a *ponderación.*

Peru's urban poor had simple sustenance and often found it cheaper and more expedient to buy prepared food from itinerant street vendors, who announced their wares at specific times of the day with different cries. Hungry customers came prepared with kitchen utensils to carry their morsels home.

The Spanish colonists' desire for wine for religious and secular consumption led to the establishment of a productive wine industry on the southern coast of Peru in the late sixteenth century. Grapes were cultivated as early as 1580 in the Moquegua Valley of the Osmore River in the far south. Wine and grape brandy (*pisco*) produced in more than 130 *bodegas* (wineries) in the valley supplied the needs of the large silver-mining center at Potosí, in present day Bolivia. Colonists also culivated grapes near the city of Villa de Valverde de Ica (Ica). Some *bodegas* exist today in the Moquegua Valley and the Ica region, continuing the four-century tradition of winemaking in this part of Peru.

On July 28, 1821, Peru declared its independence from Spain, but the Spanish didn't accede to independence until 1824, when the Viceroy finally capitulated. The status of the Indian did not improve significantly with independence. The *criollo* elite assumed the privileges of the former Spanish rulers. The struggle between the needs of the agrarian and working poor and the landed elite has led to many shifts in government, and has given rise to revolutions and economic collapses in Peru's modern history.

The African Slaves

The institution of slavery had been established in Spain since Roman times, but by the end of the fifteenth century, the black slave was the only source of servile labor.

As a matter of course, Pizarro and other Spanish explorers carried African slaves with them to their New World colonies. The slaves provided household labor, field hands for agricultural enterprises and manpower for road and bridge construction. Black slaves already tended the large gardens surrounding Lima, which provided produce for local consumption.

While the Spanish *encomenderos* also had a substantial number of Indian slaves, they were more reliant on their costly black slaves, whom they regarded as more prestigious chattel and more trustworthy than the newly conquered indigenous slaves. In 1543 the Crown limited *encomendero* control over the native population for fear that they would create an aristocracy that would usurp control of the colony. The shrinking Indian population also was a factor in the expansion of black slavery. The mortality rate of the Indian was

Ponderación, the traditional spiral-shaped iron mold used since colonial times to make crispy, deep-fried pastry swirls of the same name (see color insert for photo, fourth page, top right).

staggering, due largely to the natives' lack of immunity to germs brought by the Spanish and their livestock. Black slave trade became a large-scale enterprise as the extent of forced Indian labor decreased.

The importance of black labor to the survival of the Peruvian economy was immeasurable. In addition to their work in agricultural sectors, black slaves played a vital role in Peru's mining and wine industries. Many were trained artisans and became respected craftsmen. Black bondage in Peru lasted over 300 years. It was not abolished when Peru gained its independence from Spain in 1824. It flourished for three more decades before emancipation in 1854.

The Peruvian menu has many entries attributable to its black population. *Afroperuana* culinary contributions include the very popular appetizers or late-night street food known as *anticuchos,* pieces of beef heart, chicken hearts, or other variety meats, or fish, marinated in a spicy, vinegary mixture with red chile peppers and grilled on skewers. Other signature dishes are *morusa,* a purée of large white lima (butter) beans with sliced pork, bacon, garlic and onions; *sangrecita,* a mixture of cooked chicken blood, chile peppers and seasonings served with fresh corn kernels; *fríjol (frejol) colado,* a sweet paste of black or red beans cooked until thick with evaporated milk, brown sugar, and ground cinnamon, cloves and sesame seeds; *tacu tacu,* a mixture of leftover beans and rice, flavored with onion, garlic, chile pepper paste and pork fat, and fried into a patty or tapered tube (see recipe, p. 60); and *picarones,* a doughnut-like snack or dessert made from a yeasty pumpkin dough. The rings of dough are formed by hand, deep-fried and served with raw-sugar syrup flavored with orange, aniseed, cinnamon and cloves. African cooks adapted the Spanish recipe for *picarones,* replacing wheat flour with pumpkin purée (see recipe, p. 67). A dessert (*turrón de Doña Pepa*) created by a former slave in gratitude to the Lord of Miracles for healing her lame leg is a treat made with three thick yellow slabs of anise-flavored shortbread stuck together with honey or syrup. Sprinkled on top is a riot of colorful little candies.

The Asians

The Chinese

Peru experienced a serious labor shortage with the emancipation of the black slaves in 1854. At this time the world had an extreme shortage of fertilizer, and Peru had abundant quantities of one of the best fertilizers then known—guano. Off the coast were several islands literally blanketed with birds that feasted on the rich supply of small fish in the surrounding waters. Because rainfall in the area was essentially nonexistent, the guano deposits did not wash away; the accumulation was hundreds of feet thick. In the absence of black slave labor, Chinese workers, or coolies, were brought to the country under contract to do the miserable job of digging and sacking guano. They were typically duped into the arrangement by slavers operating out of ports in southern China. The Chinese performed many other jobs and services. The construction of a rail system across Peru in the 1860s and 1870s required massive amounts of human labor, again supplied by the Chinese. They were also field laborers, house servants, cooks, porters, factory workers and general handymen.

The Chinese influence on Peruvian cuisine has been more than sensational. What appealed was the fusion of Chinese and Peruvian flavors, not traditional Chinese cooking per se. The Chinese introduced many new ingredients, such as soy sauce and fresh ginger, and mixed them with indispensable Peruvian seasonings such as hot chile peppers. Their method of stir-fry cookery became widely used. One of the national favorites today is *lomo saltado,* marinated strips of beef stir-fried with red onion, tomatoes, red bell peppers, Peruvian yellow chile peppers (*ajíes amarillos*) and soy sauce, then tossed with French fries. Another preparation with Chinese overtones is *arroz chaufa,* a fusion dish of fried rice mixed with various Peruvian ingredients such as sausage and chile peppers. Eateries serving Chinese-Peruvian dishes, *chifas,* are enormously popular. The first were started in Lima by Chinese immigrants at the end of the 19th century. Today they are throughout Peru, but especially in coastal cities.

The Japanese

A Japanese migration to Peru commenced in 1899 with a shipload of immigrants who came to work on the cotton and sugar plantations, helping to fill Peru's need for agricultural laborers. The first Japanese restaurants appeared in Peru as early as the 1920s. The menus emphasized fish at a time when meat was more appreciated by wealthy urbanites. In time, the Japanese helped to make fish a higher-priority dietary staple and introduced a variety of new fresh fish dishes. They were instrumental in changing the status of *ceviche* from house food to restaurant fare. Perhaps their most important contribution to Peru's culinary repertoire is *tiradito,* a raw fish preparation similar to *ceviche* but characteristically made with thin, flattened slices of fish. Onions, an important component of *ceviches,* are omitted from *tiradito* dishes.

Novoandino (New Andean) Cuisine

In the early 1990s, a culinary movement inspired by food professionals Bernardo Roca Rey and Don Cucho la Rosa looked to the ancient Peruvian past to create a modern fusion cuisine that combined pre-colonial Incan (or earlier) ingredients with elements of innovative nouvelle cuisine. One such ancient ingredient prominently featured in *novoandino* inventions is quinoa, a hardy, protein-rich seed resembling a sesame seed. After quinoa is cooked, it becomes translucent and the external germ on its surface forms an opaque, incomplete ring twisted outward. *Novoandino* risottos are made with quinoa grains in place of rice and are aptly called *quinottos.* They often are served elegantly molded and garnished. Versatile quinoa is showcased in savory *novoandino* tarts comprised of stacks of little quinoa pancakes separated by a creamy fresh-spinach filling (see recipe, p. 63), and in sweet quinoa crêpes filled with cape gooseberry jam and topped with orange sauce (see recipe, p.68). Other *novoandino* dishes include guinea pig

Novoandino invention called a *quinotto,* which is made with quinoa, a protein-rich seed that becomes translucent when cooked. The name is a play on the word risotto, although the cooking process is not the same as that used to make a risotto. This molded *quinotto* contains peas, mushrooms and diced carrots.

legs, resembling little drumsticks, which are perched vertically in a sauce, and alpaca steaks embellished with French-style sauces. There appears to be no end to the delicious *novoandino* dishes we can expect to discover on menus. The possibilities afforded by the *novoandino* movement have made Peru's kitchens an exciting laboratory for chefs trained locally and abroad. And the rediscovery of ancient native crops is having a positive effect on the rural economy where the crops are produced. Good for Peru—great for tourists!

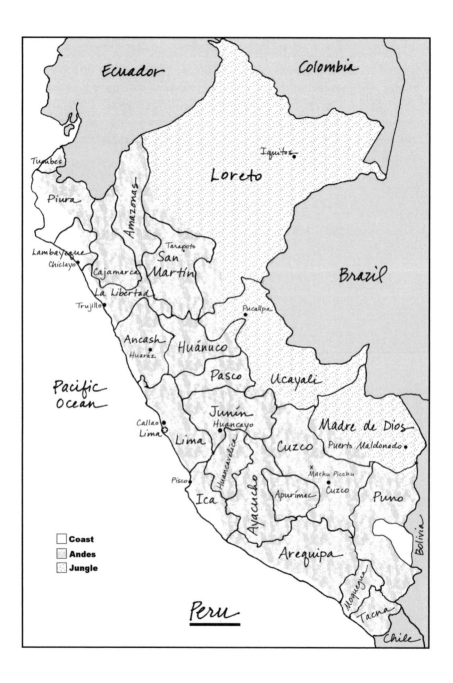

Peru

Regional Peruvian Food

A Quick Tour of Peruvian Foods and Their Regional Variations

Peruvian Food in a Nutshell

The explosive combination of flavors in Peruvian cooking creates a cuisine unlike any other. The heat of chile peppers, the tangy acidity of tropical limes, the pungent aromas of cilantro and *huacatay,* the delicate flavors of a rich variety of seafood and river fish combine with a wide variety of grains and tubers for a taste and texture sensation. Because Peru's wildly diverse geographical regions are fairly narrow strips, it has been relatively easy for coastal and jungle foods to make their way to the Andes and for the foods of the Andes to be transported to the coast and the jungle. The people have been quick to incorporate the many new foods brought by the Spanish colonists, their African slaves, and subsequent immigrants from China, Japan and elsewhere. This readiness to experiment has produced an exciting cuisine using both traditional and nouvelle ingredients and preparation methods.

Rare is the Peruvian dish that does not include chile pepper. Each river valley oasis along the western slopes of the Andes has a microclimate that produces unique varieties of chile peppers, which are, in turn, completely different from the peppers native to the jungle. Despite the availability of this enormous variety, two types of chile peppers predominate in the Peruvian kitchen. *Ají amarillo*, referred to as *ají escabeche* or *ají verde* in some parts of the country, is a finger-shaped pepper about 6 inches long that, despite its name (yellow chile pepper), is orange when ripe. Deveined, deseeded, and sometimes blanched to decrease its heat, this pepper is made into a paste that is used to flavor many sauces and soups. Strips of the fresh pepper are used in ceviches, salads and stews and as garnish in many dishes. Although *ají amarillo* certainly is a hot chili pepper, its heat doesn't overwhelm its delicate flavor and aroma. *Ají rocoto* is an apple-shaped pepper, often served as *rocoto relleno*, stuffed with a mixture of seasoned ground meat, topped with cheese and baked. Fiery hot *rocoto* peppers are particularly popular in the southern Andes near Arequipa and Cuzco. Beyond these two favorites, a few other chile peppers deserve mention for their role in Peruvian cuisine. *Ají limo*, similar to the *ají amarillo* in shape and heat, can be red, orange, green, yellow or dark purple. It often is used to add a colorful, festive look to *ceviches* and other dishes. *Ají colorado,* a dark-red chile pepper, is most often used in its dried form, *ají panca,* as a seasoning for darker sauces and soups. Powdered *ají panca* is an ingredient in the popular commercial spice mixture Sybarita. Strips of *ají dulce* (bell pepper) are featured in the popular beef stir-fry *lomo saltado.* Other peppers may be available only in particular regions. *Ají mochero,* which grows in the Moche River valley near Trujillo, is commonly used in cooking in the north. In the jungle, tiny incendiary peppers, such as the pea-sized, orange *ají charapita* and wrinkly *pucunu uchu,* are likely to be more common.

Seafood is an integral part of the Peruvian diet. The Humboldt Current, which flows from the southern tip of Chile to the northern coast of Peru, brings extremely cold waters from the Antarctic and causes an enormous upwelling of organic material from the sea floor. This nutrient-rich water supports a rich growth of plankton, which, in turn, creates the conditions for the most bountiful fisheries in the world. And whether the fish are harvested by large, international commercial fishing trawlers or in the centuries-old manner by village men astride traditional *totora* reed boats, the result is nothing short of a bonanza for the seafood lover. Peruvian cuisine is unsurpassed for the freshness and variety of its fish and shellfish.

Peru is perhaps most famous for its mouthwatering *ceviches.* The classic *ceviche* is made with bite-size chunks of extremely fresh, firm, white fish (sole or tilapia, for example), marinated in ice-cold, freshly squeezed Key lime juice just long enough to "cook" the flesh (one or two minutes), then tossed with thin slices of chile peppers (typically *ají amarillo* or *ají limo*) and red onions and served on a bed of fresh lettuce, with rounds of corn on the cob and chunks of sweet potato on the side (see recipe, p. 46). *Ceviche* is often served with an accompaniment of toasted corn kernels (*cancha*). The liquid from the *ceviche*—tangy, salty, spicy, and cold—is sometimes served on the side in shot-size glasses with a tiny spoon. The spoon is used to scoop up the crunchy *cancha* kernels and dunk them in this liquid, known as *leche de tigre* (tiger's milk). The combination of flavors is surprisingly satisfying.

Ají amarillo, the most commonly used pepper in Peru, is grown throughout the country. It has a deep orange color when ripe. Seeded peppers are used raw as a garnish, cooked with foods or made into a paste, which colors food a bright yellow besides adding piquancy.

Endless variations on the classic *ceviche* are readily available in restaurants from the neighborhood *cevicherías,* small eateries where the locals have a late morning snack made with the morning's catch, to the five-star restaurants experimenting with novel combinations of ingredients. *Ceviches* are made with many varieties and combinations of fish and shellfish. The chile peppers used may be of different colors and degrees of heat. Additional herbs (cilantro, chives, parsley) may be included. The traditional accompaniments may be varied to include a slice of steamed yuca, loose kernels of boiled corn, artichoke hearts, tomato wedges, or different types of potatoes. Mango, *camu camu* (a tiny, tart jungle fruit) or other fruit may be in the mix. To recreate pre-colonial *ceviche,* the juice of the *tumbo,* a variety of passion fruit, is sometimes used to acidify the fish in place of Key lime juice, which was only available after the Spanish brought citrus fruits to the new world. Sour orange (*naranja agria*) and even corn beer (*chicha de jora*) may be used to create the marinade. Those who don't care for seafood can enjoy *ceviches* based on mushrooms, lupine seeds (*tarwi*), duck, lizard and more!

The influence of the Japanese in Peru is seen in the popularity and variety of *tiradito* offerings. Similar to *ceviches* in the use of fresh raw fish, *tiraditos* differ in that the fish is cut in long, flattened strips, and no onions are used in the preparation. *Tiradito* sauces tend to be thicker than those used for traditional *ceviches* and may include evaporated milk. *Tiraditos* are often served with the strips of fish artfully arranged on a platter with a drizzle or stripe of the accompanying sauce across the top. Another typical presentation is to serve a mound of fish strips thoroughly mixed with the sauce.

Fresh seafood is most readily available in the coastal areas, but plentiful crayfish or river shrimp (*camarones*), lake and river trout (*trucha*), river *pejerrey,* and Amazon fish such *doncella, dorado* and the gigantic *paiche* assure that fish and shellfish are a regular part of the cuisine throughout Peru. *Pescado sudado,* white fish fillets steamed over a bed of onions and tomato, with chile peppers and cilantro, has its analog in the jungle in *pescado de patarashca,* white fish fillets steamed in banana leaf packets with tomatoes, onions, bell peppers, garlic and false cilantro (*sacha culantro*), a jungle herb with a cilantro-like flavor. *Chupe de camarones* (river shrimp chowder) is a national favorite. This cheesy chowder has chunks of white fish, potatoes, rounds of corn on the cob, poached eggs, delectable river shrimp with a mild, lobster-like flavor, and plenty of heat from the chile peppers (*ajíes amarillos*).

Although meat tends not to be a daily menu item in most Peruvian homes, the variety of meats eaten is astonishing. In addition to the beef, goat, lamb and chicken brought by the Spanish, Peruvians eat alpaca, guinea pig, duck and turkey. There is even an effort to adapt ostrich to grow in the high altitudes of the Andes. In the jungle, many wild animals, including peccary, tapir, monkeys, red deer and agouti, are hunted and eaten (legally and illegally). *Carne de monte,* a collective term referring to the meat from these jungle animals, may be offered on menus and in jungle markets, but is likely from protected species and not legal for tourist consumption. Reptiles such as turtles, tortoises and cayman are prized, as are the larvae of the palm weevil (*suri*) and the abdomens of leaf-cutter ant queens (*siquisapa*). No part of an animal is wasted. Tripe, liver, kidney, heart, hoofs, all are to be found in soups and stews. *Cau cau,* a tripe-based stew, is a national favorite. *Patasca* is a well-loved Andean soup that includes both tripe and cow's feet. Bull-nose salad (*ensalada de sencca*) is a luncheon offering in Arequipa's *picanterías.*

Beans are an important source of protein throughout Peru. The canary bean (*frijol canario*), lima bean or butter bean (*pallar*), chickpea (*garbanzo*), fava bean (*faba* or *haba*) and many varieties of lentils (*lentejas*) are used in soups, such as *chupe de pallares verdes* (see recipe, p. 51) and *shambar,* appetizers, such as *puspu* (made with fava beans), and salads and side dishes (for example, *frijol redondo;* see recipe, p. 58). The popular comfort food *tacu tacu* is a fried patty of seasoned leftover beans and rice (see recipe, p. 60). Beans are even used to make a marmalade-like dessert, *frijol colado. Tarwi,* called *chocho* in the north, is the seed of the Andean lupine (*Lupinus mutabilis*). *Tarwi* has a higher content of nutritious oils and certain essential amino acids than most other beans. As a bonus, *tarwi* flowers provide a beautiful splash of purple to the spring landscape of the Andes.

The peanut is another native legume that has an important place in the Peruvian kitchen and history. Although peanut translates to *cacahuate* in

Spanish, in Peru (and most of South America) peanuts are referred to as *maní,* from the Arawak Indian language of the Amazon basin where the peanut originated, or as *inchik,* the Quechua word for peanut. Ground, roasted peanuts are used to thicken and flavor dishes, such as *carapulcra* and some *pepiánes. Ocopa* is a classic Peruvian dish of boiled potatoes with a sauce made from ground, roasted peanuts, evaporated milk, cheese, onions, garlic, chile peppers and *huacatay* (a pungent herb). And *inchikapi* (peanut soup in Quechua) is a chicken and ground peanut soup popular in the jungle.

Corn or maize (*choclo*), a New World grain believed to have originated in what is now Mexico, is a part of many meals in Peru. It is ground to make the fillings for tamales and *humitas* and to thicken soups and *pepiánes.* Cobs of corn are sliced into rounds that are served alongside *ceviches* or used in stews. *Mote,* a broad, flat, white kernel, and *chulpe,* an elongated, teardrop-shape kernel, are both toasted and served warm and salted as an appetizer and accompaniment with *ceviches* and *picantes. Pastel de choclo,* a corn cake made with ground or grated fresh corn, is a moist, smooth, flavorful delight (see recipe, p. 56), bearing no resemblance to the granular texture of North American cornbread. One of the most important uses of corn, particularly in the Andes, is to provide the "ferment" for the corn beer *chicha de jora.*

Rarely is a Peruvian meal served without a side dish of rice (*arroz*), typically molded (*moldeado*) into a flat-topped form with a deep but narrow depression in the center. Garnishes of cilantro, parsley or other colorful vegetables are often placed in or around this central depression to provide visual interest. In the jungle, the side dish of rice is likely to give way to the side of boiled or fried sticks of yuca. Its starchy texture and somewhat bland flavor make it a useful vehicle for delivering aromatic sauces and as a thickener for stews and chowders (*espesado,* for example; see recipe, p. 65).

Quinoa (*quinua*) and amaranth (*kiwicha*) are grains native to the high altitudes and intense sunlight of the Andes. Loaded with protein and beautiful to look at, quinoa is used in

Arroz moldeado, molded rice, is served with nearly every Peruvian meal. The traditional mold is wooden with a central spindle and a convenient handle for scooping the rice.

traditional Andean cooking and is a favorite among chefs creating *novoandino* dishes. When cooked slowly with seasonings and vegetables, it absorbs moisture to create *quinotto*—a quinoa-based dish in the style of risotto (see recipe, p. 62). It is used in soups and as the basis of savory pancakes and sweet crêpes (see recipes, pp. 63 and 68, respectively, and photos in color insert, eighth page, top, and sixth page, bottom, respectively). Quinoa and amaranth are served as breakfast cereals in puffed or flaked form and ground into high-energy liquid breakfast drinks, served hot or cold. Amaranth plants look spectacular and are also welcome as ornamental garden plants. Although used less often than quinoa and amaranth, *kañiwa* is yet another protein-rich, delicious grain grown in the Andes.

Nowhere in the world do more varieties of tubers grow than in Peru, which boasts over a hundred wild varieties of potatoes in addition to thousands of cultivated types. Potatoes originated in the Andes, where the mountain peoples have cultivated varieties suited to different microclimates for about 7000 years. Peruvians have available potatoes of nearly every size, shape, color and texture imaginable, and they use those various qualities to infuse their dishes with flavor, texture and visual interest. The workhorse is the yellow potato (*papa amarilla*), sometimes known commercially as the Peruvian Gold potato. Its slightly waxy texture allows it to stand up well in soups, under sauces (for example, *papas a la huancaina*, see recipe, p. 47), baked in a potato and cheese casserole (*pastel de papas*) or served mashed and cold, layered with colorful fillings in *causa*. *Papa huayro*, a yellow potato with thin purple skin, is also very popular. Its tenderness more than makes up for the effort required to peel this knobby potato with deep eyes (see color insert, last page, bottom right). Dehydrated potato bits (*papa seca*) are an ingredient of many stews and soups, including the classic dish *carapulcra*, an Andean stew of pork, *papa seca*, ground peanuts, chile peppers, onions, garlic and cumin. Hard chips of *papa seca* are quite different from the chalky nuggets of *chuño*, a potato that has been freeze-dried using an elaborate ancient Andean technique. *Chuño* comes in both white (*chuño blanco*) and black (*chuño negro*) varieties.

Sweet potato (*camote*), which is entirely unrelated to the potato botanically, is the traditional accompaniment with *ceviche* and is served on the side with many dishes. Peruvians also use it as the basis of several popular sweets. *Dulce de camote* comprises slices of cooked sweet potato in a cinnamony raw-sugar syrup (see color insert for photo, sixth page, top left), and *camotillo* is a sweet-potato pudding. *Picarones*, fried rings of yeasty dough made with winter squash and sweet potato, are served hot with a raw-sugar syrup spiced with cinnamon, cloves, aniseed, and orange peel (see recipe, p. 67, and color insert for photo, second page, top right). Many other tubers are used regularly in Peruvian cooking and as medicinal agents. Colorful *oca* and *olluco* have thin skins and firm flesh. *Arracacha,* also known as the white carrot (*zanahoria blanca*) has a carrotlike root that tastes a bit like celery and a stalk that is eaten in salads. *Achira,* a member of the canna family, was one of the first tubers cultivated in the Andes. Its starch granules are readily extracted for use in making breads, and the leaves are used to wrap foods for cooking. *Maca,* sold in many forms as a medicinal, is touted as an aphrodisiac and source of virility and energy. The natural sweetness of the tuber *yacón* comes from sugars that aren't metabolized by humans. This member of the sunflower family thus holds great promise as a food for diabetics and as a source of a noncaloric sweetener.

While the harsh growing conditions of the Andes give rise to a plethora of tubers, the tropical climate in eastern Peru gives rise to an enormous variety of fruits, including many not typically available in North America. The *cherimoya* has green skin with several different surface patterns depending on the variety, and can be as small as an apple or as big as a cantaloupe. It has dozens of large brown seeds, each surrounded by a pocket of creamy, custardy flesh. *Aguaymanto,* the cape gooseberry or ground cherry, is a pale orange fruit the size of a cherry, encased in a papery beige husk. Tart and full of tiny seeds, *aguaymanto* is used to make sauces, syrups, and marmalade. Other jungle fruits make their way into the kitchen, including the tiny, tangy *camu camu.* This reddish-purple fruit, about the size of a grape, is supercharged with vitamin C, and is used to make juices and frozen confections. Several large Amazon fish, including the *gamitana,* feed on *camu camu,* which grows on small trees along the river. *Caimito* has a tough yellow skin and juicy, plum-like white flesh. *Cocona* is sometimes called the tomato of the jungle. At the center is a tangy, jellylike pulp, full of tiny, unnoticeable seeds. The firmer flesh surrounding the pulp is reminiscent of tomato. *Macambo*, a fruit in the *cacao* family, is large and yellow-brown with a tough, reticulated surface. Below this woody outer shell is sweet flesh that is eaten fresh or used to make juices and ice creams. The flesh surrounds large white seeds, which are toasted on skewers or fried and eaten as a snack. In jungle markets, look for all manner of bananas, from tiny, finger-size varieties to large plantains, which provide a significant portion of starch in the jungle diet.

Passion fruits abound in Peru. With its brittle shell, the *granadilla* looks like a speckled orange egg. The skin gets soft and wrinkly as the fruit ripens. Inside, the luscious, gelatinous pulp surrounds hundreds of brown seeds. Slightly larger, but with similar characteristics, is the pale-yellow *maracuyá*. The very acidic *tumbo* is an ovoid, green passion fruit, about 3 to 5 inches long. Its cousin, the *tumbo gigante,* is, indeed, gigantic—up to about 7 pounds. Passion fruits are eaten fresh and used to make juices and blended drinks, bright yellow sauces, and tasty sorbets and ice creams.

A favorite fruit among Peruvians is the fragrant *lúcuma.* Under its shiny green, leathery skin is bright orange flesh that is starchy and dry and of different degrees of sweetness, depending on the variety. In the center are one or more large, shiny brown seeds. Its teardrop shape with a ring of brown pigment around the tip is reminiscent of a female breast. Many legends surround the *lúcuma* fruit, a symbol of fertility and sexuality. Its importance is clear from the frequency with which it has been represented in pottery artifacts of successive cultures over three millennia. *Lúcuma* pulp, dried and ground, is used to make puddings, creams, icings, ice creams, sorbets, beverages, cakes and cookies.

Other fruits of the Andes include *tuna,* the bright red fruit of the prickly pear cactus, and *sacha tomate* (false tomato) or *tomatillo,* also called *tomate de árbol* (tree tomato). The ovoid fruit looks much like a purplish plum tomato, but it has a piquant flavor. Puréed with fiery *rocoto* peppers and some garlic, *sacha tomate* creates a *salsa* that leaves no taste bud unfired. *Pepino dulce* (or simply *pepino*), the cucumber melon, is round, 2–4 inches in diameter, and has smooth, pale-yellow skin with distinctive purple stripes. The flesh is

The *aguaymanto* also is called *cereza del Perú,* the cherry of Peru. In English it is known as the ground cherry, cape gooseberry and goldenberry. Tart and juicy, this berry makes a delicious marmalade, which is used in desserts and sauces.

watery and slightly sweet, with a cucumber flavor. Elderberry (*sauco*), seldom used in the North American kitchen, is much appreciated in Peru in marmalades and both sweet and savory sauces.

Central to many *criolla* dishes, second only to the *ají amarillo,* is the tropical lime. Called *limón* in Peru, this hardworking citrus fruit is neither the lemon nor the lime familiar to North Americans. Perhaps its closest familiar kin is the Key lime. The tropical lime is small—perhaps an inch in diameter. Its acidic juice lacks the spiciness of the North American lime and the face-puckering power of the North American lemon. It is the perfect refreshing balance to the heat of the chile peppers used in nearly every dish. Sticklers use only fresh-squeezed *jugo de limón* and eschew the use of juice presses, which release bitter oils from the rind. The tropical lime is a key ingredient of the *pisco sour* (see recipe, p. 43) and most *ceviches.*

Most of the vegetables in the Peruvian kitchen are similar to those found in North America. Tomatoes, carrots, peas, green beans, broccoli, cauliflower, avocado, onions, scallions, lettuce, artichokes and asparagus are all familiar. But a number of vegetables are less familiar to North Americans, including the many varieties of chile peppers described earlier and several types of squash. *Zapallo* is a large (up to 30 pounds!), round squash that looks like a green-skinned pumpkin. These enormous squash are sold by the slice in markets. *Loche* (or *zapallo loche*) is about a foot long, with dark green skin. The flesh is firm and yellow-orange with no seeds. Grated *loche* is included in many stews and *secos,* thickening the sauces without overwhelming the other flavors. A reasonable substitute for *loche* in recipes is the butternut squash. *Caigua* (*caihua, caygua*) is a squash of an entirely different type. Its pale-green, undulating surface has subtle, dark-green striations and a bent tip. This hollow squash has crisp, juicy flesh that makes it perfect for stuffing. *Caigua* is an ingredient of many soups and stews and is also eaten fresh, particularly in salads.

Onion, garlic, chile peppers and cilantro are the most common seasonings (other than salt and pepper, of course). Oregano, cumin, parsley and *palillo,* a turmeric-like native root, also feature prominently. In the jungle, *sacha culantro* (false cilantro) is often used to obtain a cilantro-like flavor, although the herbs are botanically unrelated. *Huacatay* (*Tagetes minuta*) is a native Peruvian herb in the marigold family that is used fresh to season many sauces and marinades. *Huacatay* is sometimes referred to as black mint in English, although it is neither black, nor discernibly minty. *Hierbabuena* (*yerbabuena*) is a true mint that also makes its way into many Peruvian dishes. The *molle* tree bears beautiful wisteria-like bunches of reddish-pink fruits that dry into pink peppercorns, which are ground and used as a seasoning.

A good beverage complements a good meal, and Peru has unique drinks suited to any palate. Bright blue and yellow billboards and signs advertise the national soft drink, *Inca Kola*. This extremely sweet, almost fluorescent yellow, carbonated beverage is much more popular than regular colas in Peru. Purées of fresh fruits, which may be mixed with yogurt or milk (*batidos*), are a healthy alternative. *Chicha morada* is a nonalcoholic beverage made by boiling dried purple corn on the cob with pineapple rind, dried fruits, cinnamon and cloves. The dark purple liquid is strained, sweetened and served chilled with finely chopped bits of pineapple and apple in the glass (see recipe, p. 44). *Chicha morada* also can be allowed to ferment before serving. Peru grows some of the finest coffee in the world. Paradoxically, it can be difficult to find a good cup of coffee in Peru because most of the best coffee is exported. Teas typically offered include *té puro* (black tea), *té manzanilla* (chamomile) and *mate de coca* (coca tea), which is recommended for avoiding altitude sickness when traveling in the Andes.

Among alcoholic beverages, *chicha de jora* is the classic. This Andean brew is made from fermented corn in small batches in individual homes and small establishments. Peru has two major brands of beer (*cerveza*), Cusqueña and Arequipeña. *Llonque,* an unrefined brandy distilled from sugar cane, is a popular spirit (*aguardiente*). But the *pisco sour,* considered the national cocktail, is made with the colorless Peruvian grape brandy *pisco,* Key lime

Basket of artfully arranged *caigua*. The hollow, pale-green, mild-flavored squash is served fresh in salads, cooked in soups or stuffed and baked.

juice, egg whites and sugar syrup (see recipe, p. 43). Variations are made using *pisco* with macerated fruits or herbs (such as coca leaves). Although most of the grapes grown in the Ica Valley in southern coastal Peru go to making *pisco,* this area has a thriving wine industry, and Peruvian wines are readily available.

The Regions of Peru

Peru's three natural geographical zones—coast, mountains, jungle—also provide a logical framework for discussing regional variations in the cuisine. We will further subdivide the coastal zone into the north coast, Lima and environs, and the south coast, in part because most of the population and the largest cities are located along the coast.

The North Coast

The north coast covers an area north of Lima to the Ecuador border, and from the Pacific Ocean in the west into the western foothills of the Andes to the east. It includes parts of the departments of Tumbes, Piura, Lambayeque, La Libertad and Ancash and the major cites of Piura, Chiclayo and Trujillo. Most of this land is a treeless desert interspersed with fertile valleys surrounding rivers that originate in the Andes. Agriculture is confined to the irrigated areas near these valleys. The sea provides fish and shellfish.

Along the far north coast, the department of Tumbes is known for its lovely beach resorts situated on the small portion of Peru's coastline not fed by the frigid waters of the Humboldt Current. Just to the south of Tumbes is the department of Piura. Like Tumbes, Piura has beautiful resort beaches, although, with the exception of years when El Niño brings warmer waters to the coast, the Humboldt Current assures that the ocean is quite chilly. The lowest pass through the Peruvian Andes (Paso de Porculla) is in Piura. Because of this relatively easy connection between the jungle and the sea, the Piura region has been an important cultural and commercial crossroads. Continuing south along the coast is the department of Lambayeque and its capital, Chiclayo, the third largest city outside the metropolitan Lima area. La Libertad, home to the city of Trujillo, and Ancash lead to Lima.

Seafood is, naturally, central to the coastal diet. Mangrove swamps along the northern coast of Tumbes provide an exclusive breeding ground for black scallops (*conchas negras*), which are the star of the menu here. *Ceviches* and stews feature black scallops. *Aguadito,* a chunky soup typically made with fowl (hen or duck), grains, potatoes and broth, is made with black scallops in Tumbes. Other shellfish, such as crabs, oysters and shrimp, also feature prominently in the north-coast cuisine. *Ají de langostinos,* shrimp in a creamy yellow sauce flavored with chili peppers, is a favorite. *Cangrejo revantado* is made with fresh small crabs smashed atop a mixture of diced boiled potato, sautéed onion, garlic, chile peppers and seaweed, cooked with egg and wine or corn beer. In the fishing community of Huanchaco, just north of Trujillo, local fishermen still fish in traditional *caballitos* ("little horses"), *totora* reed boats, although modern *caballitos* include Styrofoam blocks to assist with flotation. Restaurants in Huanchaco serve fresh seafood in classic forms, including *pescado sudado*—fillets of white fish steamed over layers of onions and tomatoes with slices of the *ají amarillo,* herbs and spices. (See recipe, p. 55, and color insert for photo, seventh page, bottom.) Two types of dried fish are popular in the markets and restaurants of Chiclayo and the north coast, in general. Dried guitar fish (*guitarra*) is the basis of *chinguirito,* a signature *ceviche* of the Chiclayo area. *Tortilla de raya,* an omelet-like pancake of beaten egg with vegetables and pieces of dried ray, is another favorite in the department of Lambayeque.

Two soups are standout first courses in the north, particularly Trujillo. *Sopa teóloga* (or *sopa teológica*) is made with meat from a turkey or chicken hen. Lentils, tomatoes, onions, chile pepper and other seasonings flavor the soup, while saffron, turmeric or a turmeric-like native root, *palillo,* make it yellow. *Sopa teóloga* is served with rice and, like many other dishes in Peru, typically is garnished with quartered hard-boiled eggs and sliced olives. *Shambar* is another fabulous soup, which, while enjoyed throughout Peru, typically is on the Monday menu in Trujillo. Thick with wheat berries, lentils and other beans, the soup is also flavored by ham bones and chile peppers, with refreshing cilantro and mint.

Arroz con pato is a classic dish of the Chiclayo region. Pieces of duck are cooked in dark beer (or *chicha*) with onions, garlic, chile peppers (*ajíes amarillos*) and other vegetables. The duck is served with rice mixed with peas and colored green by large amounts of chopped cilantro. *Espesado,* a beef stew with a cilantro-flavored sauce thickened with ground corn, yuca and grated winter squash (see recipe, p. 65), typically is served with rice and yuca.

Goat and kid (suckling goat) are readily available in northern Peru and featured in some of the classic dishes that might be made with lamb in other parts of Peru. In *seco de cabrito* pieces of kid meat are cooked slowly in a thick sauce made with grated vegetables (carrots and winter squash), cilantro, garlic, onions, and corn beer (*chicha de jora*). This dish, also called *cabrito a la norteña* (northern-style kid), is usually served over rice with a side of beans (see recipe, p. 58, and photo in color insert, third page, top left).

Chirimpico, a Chiclayo favorite, is a stew made with kid tripe (and sometimes other organ meats) and grated winter squash (*loche*), flavored with garlic, onion, chile peppers, cilantro and Key lime juice. It usually is served with boiled yuca and sweet potatoes. Goat cheese is an ingredient of the Piuran dish *mala rabia* (literally, "evil rage"). The various components of the dish— rice, peas, mashed ripe bananas mixed with crumbled fresh goat cheese, and cubes of dried fish in a mixture of *chicha de jora* and corn vinegar (*vinagre de chicha*)—are arranged separately on a single platter. *Natillas,* a pudding made with goat's milk, unrefined sugar (*chancaca*) and rice flour, is another Piuran classic.

The northern cooking style often includes marinating meat or fish in *chicha* and using *chicha* or *vinagre de chicha* as part of the cooking liquid or sauce. Although *chicha de jora* is most common, *chicha* is made from a wide variety of grains, fruits and vegetables. The importance of *chicha* historically and culturally is hard to overestimate. In ancient times it was used solely for ceremonial purposes. With time, and with the development of ceramics that

Totora reed boats "racked" for the day on the beach in Huanchaco, just north of Trujillo. The boats are called *caballitos* or little horses, because fishermen "ride" them out to sea to tend their fishing nets.

allowed for brewing and storing larger amounts of *chicha,* its use spread to include social imbibing. The Spanish conquerors failed in their attempts to ban the use of *chicha,* in part because of the deep religious significance attached to it. Today, *chicha* is still made in relatively small batches and served from homes and *chicherías,* small, local establishments that make and serve *chicha.* A small red flag attached to a pole outside a door or window signals that the establishment has a batch of *chicha* available.

Forests of carob or locust bean trees (*algarroba*) grow on the edges of the Sechura desert in Piura and Lambayeque. These highly adaptable, drought-resistant leguminous trees return nitrogen to the soil and provide wood for charcoal and building crafts. The trees produce large pods of beans with myriad uses. They are used locally as feed for livestock (mainly goats). The sweet pulp in the fresh pods is eaten. The beans are a source of locust gum for the food preapration industry. Dried pods are ground to make carob powder and syrup. Carob, sometimes used as a substitute for chocolate, lacks the psychoactive properties of cocoa, and is used both as a flavorant and as a health supplement. The *algarrobina* is a delicious cocktail made with *pisco,* milk, egg, sugar, carob syrup and nutmeg (see recipe, p. 44).

Rivers originating in the Andes cut through the coastal desert, creating valleys of the same names. Dams and irrigation harness the fresh waters of these rivers to create highly productive agricultural areas, primarily growing rice, cotton, sugar cane, sorghum, tropical limes and, particularly farther north, bananas and coconut.

A dish typical of the far northern department of Tumbes is banana ball soup (*caldo de bolas de banana*), which is made from green bananas (plantains) that are cooked and mashed, then formed into balls around a stuffing of finely chopped ground meat, onions, tomatoes, raisins, boiled eggs and olives. The banana balls are served with potatoes in a meat-based broth. In Piura, a favorite dish is *seco de chavelo,* which combines grilled plantains with pieces of salted, dried meat (*cecina*) in a sauce made with sautéed garlic, onions, tomatoes, cumin, chile pepper (*ají panca*), salt and vinegar. Bananas also are made into *chifles,* a delicious snack food. Slices of green banana or plantain are boiled briefly, then smashed flat and deep-fried. Sweet or savory seasonings or accompanying sauces add variety to the taste of the *chifles.* A popular cocktail is the *chinguirito* (not to be confused with the special *ceviche* of the same name), made with *pisco* and coconut water. *Antecoco,* a sweet paste made with coconut, milk and sugar, is the signature dessert of Tumbes.

Sugar cane is one of the biggest agricultural crops of northern coastal Peru. Some is refined into sugar, but much is also made into raw sugar (*chancaca*), which is sold in molded blocks. In markets, *chancaca* blocks typically are wrapped in banana or other large leaves, or in brown paper. *Chancaca* adds a rich, molasses-type flavor to syrups and sauces. Many Peruvian desserts use a sweet milk caramel (*manjar blanco*) as a filling or topping. *Alfajores,* flaky sandwich cookies with *manjar blanco* filling, came to Peru from the Moors courtesy of Spanish nuns, who brought their recipes for *alfajores* and many other pastries to Peru when they established convents. The trademark dessert of Lambayeque, the *King Kong,* may be thought of as *alfajores* on steroids. This gargantuan treat lives up to its name. It has enormous cookies layered with fillings of *manjar blanco,* sweet peanut cream or a variety of fruit pastes (quince, fig or pineapple). *King Kongs* are made round or square, with soft or crunchy cookies, a single filling or multiples fillings. They are sold by street vendors and in small shops, particularly in Chiclayo and Trujillo (see color insert, last page, bottom left).

Lima and Environs

Lima, the capital of Peru, is situated in the Rímac River valley, approximately halfway down the coast. Lima is a department unto itself. The adjacent port of Callao is a separate administrative district, but for practical purposes, it is a suburb of Lima. Lima's population has grown dramatically with the influx of rural people seeking a better life in the city. Of course, the dream comes true for only a few; the rest live in the ever-expanding slums of Lima in conditions far worse than what they sought to escape.

For tourists and those with money, Lima offers a fantastic opportunity to savor cuisines from around the world. North Americans eager for a taste of home will find pizzerias and fast-food chains such as McDonald's and KFC. *Limeñans* like to get their fast food at *pollerías* and *brasserías,* where seasoned chickens are grilled or roasted to succulent perfection on a rotisserie in special brick ovens. *Cevicherías* offer a quick late-morning snack or lunch of fresh seafood "cooked" in lime juice and flavored with onions and chile peppers.

As in any major urban center, Lima has restaurants specializing in many foreign cuisines. The busy Chinatown area has a wide selection of *chifas,* restaurants specializing in Chinese food with a distinct Peruvian slant. Many fine restaurants specialize in traditional Peruvian favorites and home foods: appetizers of *ceviche* and *anticuchos* (spicy chunks of marinated beef heart grilled on skewers); main courses of *ají de gallina* (shredded chicken in a thick, milk-based, sauce made with chile peppers and ground walnuts; see recipe, p. 65), *lomo saltado* (marinated strips of beef stir-fried with red onion, tomatoes, red bell peppers and *ajíes amarillos,* then tossed with hot French fries; see color insert for photo, eighth page, middle), *chonchitas a la parmesana* (scallops broiled on the half shell with butter and Parmesan cheese), *tacu tacu* (leftover beans and rice mixed with pork fat and seasonings, then fried into a patty), *rocotos rellenos* (fiery hot *rocoto* peppers stuffed with savory meat filling, topped with cheese and baked) and *huatia* (meat cooked slowly with herbs in a sealed clay pot; see recipe, p. 61, and cover photo).

Causa, often called *causa limeña,* is a traditional dish with variations limited only by the imagination of the cook. The essential ingredient of *causa* is cold mashed potatoes flavored with chile peppers, onions, Key lime juice and other seasonings. The mashed potatoes are layered with fillings such as seafood, chicken salad or avocado. A *causa* may be made as an individual serving using a round mold. It may be made like a jellyroll, with a layer of cold mashed potatoes taking the place of the cake, served in slices. It may be made like a layer cake, served in wedges. In the home it may be made in a square or rectangular pan and cut in squares like a lasagna. A *causa* may have one filling or several. The mashed potatoes may be brightly colored, using purple potatoes (for blue), *ají amarillo* chile peppers (for yellow) or cilantro or spinach to color yellow potatoes (for green). The top of the *causa* is often elaborately decorated with olives, colored mayonnaises, chile peppers, boiled eggs or sprigs of cilantro or parsley. This versatile and festive dish typically is served for lunch or as an afternoon snack and often is found on buffet tables. See p. 45 for a recipe for *causa de pulpa de cangrejo,* a *causa* made with fillings of crab meat and avocado, pictured on the first page of the color insert, top right. Another *causa, causa con pulpo al olivo,* is pictured on the fifth page of the color insert, top left.

Lima is home to the schools that train the nation's chefs and other tourist professionals and has been at the heart of the *novoandino* movement. Many restaurants now specialize in this fusion of pre-colonial ingredients—what scientists on the National Research Council have called "The Lost Crops of the Incas"—with nouvelle cuisine techniques and European-style sauces. Grains such as quinoa and amaranth, fruits such as *sacha tomate, camu camu, cocona, aguaymanto* (cape gooseberry), *sauco* (elderberry) and *tumbo,* and tubers such as *oca* or *olluco* are brought together with seafood, guinea pig or alpaca meat, and always chile peppers in innovative New Andean dishes.

Anticuchos are pieces of beef heart marinated in a very hot chile-pepper sauce, skewered and grilled as an appetizer or late-night snack. Enjoy *anticuchos* with a *pisco sour*!

On the streets of Lima and other Peruvian cities, vendors offer many delicious fresh foods to be eaten on the go. Caution is always recommended in buying street food, a recommendation from a trusted local resident is advised. *Humitas* and *tamales,* kept warm in moist banana leaves, often are sold in the mornings. Small bags of tiny quail eggs provide an afternoon snack for hurried business people. Women sit before kettles of hot fat making doughnut-like *picarones,* served with flavored sugar syrup. Another sweet treat is a *churro,* a ridged cruller, usually filled with sweet milk caramel (*manjar blanco*). The ridges along a *churro* make it look a bit like an ear of corn. Fiery hot *anticuchos,* marinated morsels of beef heart (or other meat or fish) skewered and grilled, can take the edge off a cool, damp Lima evening. After a show or a movie, *Limeñans* may stop by drive-up stands for *butifarra,* moist, spicy pork thinly sliced and piled on rolls with *salsa criolla,* a traditional mixture of red onions, chile peppers, lime juice and salt (see recipe, p. 70).

The South Coast

South of Lima along the coast are the departments of Ica, Arequipa, Moquegua and Tacna. The desert is again punctuated by river valleys providing the moisture necessary for agriculture. Here one sees groves of Azapa, Alfonso and Arauco olive trees, providing olives for domestic use and for export around the world. Large, commercial asparagus-growing operations provide the tasty spears for North American and European markets. Vineyards in southern coastal Peru, particularly in the Ica and Moquegua valleys, provide the grapes for the Peruvian wine industry and for *pisco,* the colorless brandy that has been made here since the early 1600s. *pisco* is used in many Peruvian cocktails, including the signature *pisco sour* and the carob-flavored *algarrobina* (see recipes, pp. 43 and 44, respectively).

The community of Chincha in the department of Ica is rich in *afroperuano* culture. Many descendents of African slaves brought by the Spanish colonists live in the Chincha area, contributing music, dance, language and culinary traditions that reflect the fusion of the African and Peruvian cultures. *Carapulcra* is one of the dishes associated with this area. This delicious stew of pork (and sometimes chicken) and dried potatoes (*papa seca*), flavored with ground, roasted peanuts, onion, garlic, cumin and chile peppers is a colonial modification of an ancient Andean dish. In the Chincha area it often is served with *sopa seca,* a "dry soup" of pasta, vegetables and cheese. A purée of butter beans with roast pork or beef, *morusa,* is another main dish typical of Chincha. In the dessert department, freshly cooked *picarones,* pumpkin-based "doughnuts" are served with a syrup made from raw sugar (*chancaca*) flavored with cinnamon, cloves and aniseed, that is chin-dripping good. (See recipe, p. 67, and photo in color insert, second page, top right.) *Chapanas* and *fríjol colada* are two other favorites. *Chapanas* are dessert "tamales" made with a dough of sweetened grated yuca, sugar-cane brandy, raisins, annatto and cloves. Banana slices are stuffed inside a handful of dough, which is wrapped in banana leaves and steamed. *Fríjol colado* is a sweet paste of black beans cooked with evaporated milk, brown sugar, ground cinnamon and cloves, and then topped with toasted sesame seeds.

In addition to these *afroperuana* specialties of the Chincha area, the southern coast of Peru is known for *chupe de pallares verdes,* a chowder with lima beans, potatoes, spaghetti, corn, dried Asian shrimp, eggs, chile

Tejas are festive and delicious candies with a rich tradition in Ica.

peppers and non-melting cheese (see recipe, p. 41). *Pastel de choclo* or corn cake, is a sweet and tender dish, made with freshly grated or ground corn mixed with egg and milk layered over a mixture of seasoned ground pork and raisins and baked. And, for a sweet treat, *tejas* have a long tradition in Ica. *Manjar blanco* (sweet milk caramel) is stuffed with pieces of dried fruit or nuts, then dipped in chocolate or fondant to create fabulous candies, which are individually wrapped in fringed paper that is twisted closed on one end to create a festive package.

The Andes

The Andes mountains run the entire length of Peru. All but four of the departments of Peru—even those along the coast—are primarily in this *sierra* zone. Only Lambayeque in the northwest and the departments of Loreto, Ucayali and Madre de Dios in the east are not mainly mountainous.

The diet in the Andes makes liberal use of the many root crops that grow in the harsh conditions of the Andes. These include thousands of varieties of potatoes as well as *arracacha, achira, oca, olluco, yacón* and *maca.* Grains such as quinoa and amaranth grow here and are used as cereals, side dishes, in soups and to make hearty drinks. Guinea pig, pig, sheep and alpaca provide most of the meat that is eaten, although beans such as *tarwi* are more likely to be the primary source of protein. Freshwater shrimp (*camarones*) and fish from the mountain lakes and rivers—*trucha* (trout) and *pejerrey*—are also plentiful in many areas.

The traditional *pachamanca,* a pre-colonial Andean specialty, is still popular today. From the Quechua words *pacha* (earth) and *manca* (cooking vessel), the *pachamanca* pays tribute to *Pacha Mama* (Mother Earth) by returning the food she produces to the earth to be cooked. Special volcanic rocks that can be heated to extremely high temperatures line the bottom of a pit. Potatoes and other tubers, meats, corn and other vegetables, as well as *humitas* or *tamales* are layered with hot stones and wet banana leaves or cloths, and then sealed in the pit to allow the food to roast, absorbing the flavor of the earth. The *pachamanca* typically is made in the early months of the year to celebrate the harvest, but it is also a meal to celebrate community social events— weddings, anniversaries and religious festivals. *Huatia,* meat roasted in a sealed clay pot (*olla*) with herbs and vegetables (see recipe, p. 61, and cover photo), originally cooked in a *pachamanca,* today is cooked in the home oven.

Stews and casseroles, hearty and hot to combat the frigid climate, are the staples of the Andean menu. *Adobo de chancho,* pork marinated and stewed in *vinagre de chicha* with onions, tomatoes, chile peppers and spices, is a favorite. *Patasca,* a soup based on tripe, cow's feet and corn, appears in many variations throughout the Andes. *Hualpa chupe,* a fragrant blend of chicken, chile peppers and achiote, is a soup from the Huancayo region. *Locro,* a casserole with pre-colonial Andean origins, today is made with winter squash, potatoes, corn, onion, garlic, chile peppers, milk, cheese and chicken or meat, if it is available. *Olluquito,* another national favorite, is made from finely julienned bits of the Andean tuber *olluco* (also called *ulluco,* and *melloco*) sauteed with onions, garlic and chile peppers and cooked with meat. The shredded *olluco* and other ingredients for this dish are often sold in markets layered attractively in a tightly tied narrow plastic bag, for quick and easy preparation. A traditional Inca stew called *chuño cola* is typical of Cuzco. It is made with sausage, rice, chickpeas and potatoes and is thickened with flour made from *chuño,* potatoes freeze-dried using an ancient Andean technique. A piece of alpaca jerky (*charqui*) is usually served with *chuño cola.* *Ch'airo* is an Andean soup made with freeze-dried black potatoes (*chuño negro*) and as much meat (typically lamb intestines, dried mutton or alpaca) as a family can spare. The soup includes other starchy ingredients, such as peas, fava beans, barley, wheat berries or corn, and root crops such as carrots or turnips.

Alpaca and llama meat are tasty, low in fat, and lighter colored than beef. For centuries these camelid meats have been dried and seasoned to keep without refrigeration in a form called *charqui* (jerky). Pieces of deep-fried pork, *chicharrones de chancho,* are a favorite in the Andes, usually served with fresh or toasted kernels of corn (*choclo* or *cancha*). *Chicharrones* are prepared differently in different parts of the Andes. In the north, they may be seasoned with *ají colorado* and called *chicharrones colorado.* Tourists and other travellers through the village of Saylla near Cuzco, will likely encounter villagers wearing white stovepipe hats selling their deep-fried cubes of pork with the skin still attached (*chicharrones y tocto de Saylla*).

Although many North Americans consider guinea pigs as pets and thus are repulsed at the thought of having one for lunch, for Andean people the *cuy* has been a valued source of meat for centuries. The signature dish of Cuzco, *chiriuchi,* is served for the festival of Corpus Christi nine weeks after Easter (in June). This cold plate is a smorgasbord of favorites: roasted guinea pig and other meats, toasted corn (*cancha*), chunks of cheese (*queso andino*), and omelets (*tortillas de huevos*). Bred to have smaller litters that grow to larger adult size, *cuy* often are raised in the kitchens of the restaurants that serve them. Restaurants (*cuyerías*) specialize in baking guinea pig (*cuy al horno*) in special outdoor clay ovens. *Cuyerías* line the main street of Tipón, a village near Cuzco. Whether served up with a spicy peanut sauce (*picante de cuy*), fried crisp under a flat stone (*cuy chactado*), presented atop a bed of potatoes cooked in a chile-pepper sauce (*ajíaco de cuy*), baked and stuffed (*cuy relleno*) or made *novoandino*-style with the thigh meat pulled down over the lower leg to make tiny "drumsticks" coated in quinoa or sesame seeds, *cuy* is a favorite in the Andes. Mmm... tastes like chicken!

Huancayo is home to *papas a la huancaina,* a classic appetizer or light lunch eaten throughout Peru. A smooth yellow sauce, made with cheese, milk, cracker crumbs and chile peppers, is served cold over potatoes on a bed of lettuce, garnished with olives and slices of boiled egg (see recipe, p. 47).

Farther south, in the Arequipa area, the *rocoto* pepper is used to great advantage, most commonly as *rocoto relleno,* stuffed with a mixture of spiced ground meat, then topped with cheese and baked. *Ocopa* is the signature dish of Arequipa—boiled potatoes smothered in a sauce of milk, cheese, ground, roasted peanuts and *rocoto* peppers. Some preparations include ground shrimp or *huacatay* (a pungent herb). *Pan de tres puntas,* a roll designed to be reminiscent of the three mountains surrounding Arequipa, is eaten with cheese and cold meat or stuffed with *escribano,* a cold salad of potatoes, tomatoes, *rocoto* peppers, oil and vinegar. Served with *adobo,* it makes a great sponge for soaking up every last drop of the tasty cooking sauce.

The Jungle

The eastern slopes of the Andes, known as the brow of the jungle, descend into the jungle basins of the Amazon River and its tributaries. There are few cities in eastern Peru: Iquitos in the department of Loreto; Tarapoto in San Martín; Pucallpa in

Rocoto relleno, a specialty of Arequipa, is a very hot *rocoto* pepper stuffed with a savory meat filling, topped with cheese and baked.

Ucayali; and Puerto Maldonado in Madre de Dios. These were established primarily by the rubber industry in its heyday.

A visit to an open-air market in any of these cities showcases the astonishing bounty of the jungle, with so many varieties of fruits and chile peppers that even the vendors don't always know their names. Chefs in the jungle use these fruits to great advantage in sauces and salads, drinks and desserts. And though the ocean is far away, the rivers of the jungle teem with delicious fish. The *paiche* is so huge (about 6 feet long) that the flesh is typically salted, dried and sold rolled up like a jellyroll. The golden *dorado,* the gorgeous stiped *doncella,* and the armored *carachama* are readily available, as are river shrimp (*camarones*). Fish cooked *a la patarashca*—steamed with onion, garlic and false cilantro (*sacha culantro*) in banana leaves—is exquisite.

Tamales and *humitas* are common fare, but the *juane* is the super-size jungle version. The fillings differ, but typically include rice, yuca, or hearts of palm mixed with herbs and seasonings (onions, garlic, false cilantro, chile peppers) and some beaten egg. Two large leaves from the heliconium plant (*hojas de bijau*) are crisscrossed. A generous portion of the filling is placed in the center, topped with meat, fish, shrimp, olives, boiled egg slices or some other treat, and covered with another portion of filling. The leaves are brought up around the filling to make a melon-size package. The ends of the leaves are folded over and secured with a piece of kitchen twine or a palm fiber. As the *juane* cooks in boiling water, the fragrant aroma of the *hojas de bijau* permeates the filling.

The name "*juane*" hails from the days when Catholic missionaries made St. John the Baptist (*San Juan Bautista*) the patron saint of the Amazon River. The indigenous people, taken by the vivid image of King Herod presenting Salome with the head of *Juan Bautista* on a plate, reinvented the *juane* as a representation of the saint's head. Today they are a central feature of the June 24th festival of *San Juan Bautista* in communities throughout the jungle.

The melon-size *juane* is a jungle-style tamale named for *San Juan Bautista,* patron saint of the Amazon. It is eaten for breakfast or lunch.

A meal served *a la loretana* (from the department of Loreto) typically is served with fried yuca, fried plantains and a palm heart salad. Most dishes will incorporate at least one of these items. Yuca, fried or steamed, tends to supplant potatoes or quinoa as the starch of choice (although a mound of rice, *arroz moldeado,* still accompanies most meals). Baked goods that might have been made with wheat or rice flour elsewhere may be made with yuca flour in the jungle. Plantains, cooked, mashed with some lard and deep-fried, are the chief ingredient of the tasty appetizer or snack called *tacacho.* Pieces of salted, dried meat (*cecina*) may be included in the mash or served on the side along with a spicy, peanut-flavored dipping sauce (*inchikuchu*). Plantains also appear as *tostones* or *patacones,* twice-fried plantain slices.

The *pijuayo* and *aguaje* are extremely important natural resources in the Amazon. *Pijuayo,* the peach palm, grows to a height of about 40 or 45 feet. Its trunk is covered in strong, sharp spikes of different lengths. The trunk and leaves have uses as building materials. The tender young shoot at the top of the trunk is the source of hearts of palm (*chonta* or *palmito*). *Pijuayo* trees need to grow for about a year and a half before they are large enough to harvest for *chonta.* Commercial plantations grow *pijuayo* palms for *chonta* production under strict supervision to assure environmental protection. Fresh shoots sold in markets are shaved into long, thin ribbons, which are served atop greens to create the elegant *ensalada de chonta. Juane de chonta* has a filling of mashed hearts of palm blended with onion, garlic, toasted ground peanuts, ground corn, beaten egg, bell pepper, false cilantro and other herbs. Pieces of *paiche* or a few shrimp are included before the *juane* is wrapped up in heliconium leaves and boiled.

Pijuayo palms begin fruiting when they are about two years old. Adult *pijuayo* palms produce 6 to 8 influorescences or "stems" of flowers, each of which eventually bears 10 to 120 fruits. When ripe, the ovoid *pijuayo* fruits are 1–2 inches long and a vivid red, with areas of yellow, orange or green. The bright orange flesh is cooked and eaten like bread. It can also be dried and ground into flour, or fermented and used to make the beverage *masato.* The seed inside is spiny, like the trunk of the palm.

Another important palm is the *aguaje.* A hard, scaly skin covers the dark orange flesh. In markets *aguaje* fruits typically are sold by the bagful, already peeled. The flesh is eaten fresh, usually after being soaked in water to soften it. In Iquitos, ice cream and other frozen confections made from *aguaje* fruits are very popular, as is the beverage *aguajina. Aguaje* fruits can also be pressed for oil. Each fruit has one to three seeds, which are often eaten by children.

The fronds of the *aguaje* palm have tough fibers, which are used in textiles and to make cords and ropes. The wood can be used for construction, although it tends to be somewhat soft. The larvae of the palm weevil, which feed on rotting trunks of *aguaje* palms, are harvested and eaten fried as a delicacy (*suri*).

Palm trees are a valuable commodity for the people of the jungle. However, they are under severe threat. Harvesting the enormous "branches" of *pijuayo* fruits is a daunting challenge because of the long sharp spikes on the trunk. Likewise, the slippery trunks of the much taller *aguaje* palms make them difficult to scale. To avoid the hazards of climbing the tree, many jungle residents simply chop down the trees to harvest the fruits. This short-sighted practice has greatly reduced the wild population of *pijuayo* and *aguaje* palms in the Amazon. Many jungle animals, such as the peccary and the tapir, and Amazon fish rely on palm fruits as a nutritional source. These creatures, already under pressure from reduced habitat and poaching, suffer tremendously from the decimation of the wild palm population. But a heavily laden tree can produce enough fruits to bring a few months' income in the market, so the temptation is great for a large family living in poverty. Conservation agencies are working hard to establish programs of sustainable agriculture that can meet the needs of the local population, the local politicians, and those looking to protect the habitat.

Golden yellow, orange, red, or reddish brown, *cocona,* the tomato of the jungle, has distinctive sepals attached to the stem. The flesh is cream-colored except for some yellow pulp in the center.

Tastes of Peru

You are encouraged to prepare some of these delicious, traditional and *novoandino* (new Andean) Peruvian recipes before leaving home. This is a wonderful and immediately satisfying way to preview the extraordinary cuisine of Peru. Most of the special ingredients needed to make these dishes can be obtained in the United States in Latino and specialty food markets or can be ordered online or by mail (see *Resources*, p. 73). Satisfactory substitutes are given for those that are unavailable.

BEVERAGES/DRINKS

Pisco Sour

Pisco sour. Serves 2.

This recipe for the national drink of Peru was contributed by Roxanna Freundt de Salaverry and Alberto Salaverry, owners of Manos Morenas Restaurante in the Barranco neighborhood of Lima. Manos Morenos serves typical Peruvian food accompanied by live performances of traditional music and dance.

> ½ CUP GRANULATED SUGAR
>
> 3 TABLESPOONS WATER
>
> 2 TABLESPOONS FRESHLY SQUEEZED KEY LIME JUICE
>
> 1 EGG WHITE
>
> 3 OUNCES *PISCO**
>
> 5 ICE CUBES
>
> 1 DROP OF ANGOSTURA BITTERS

Dissolve sugar in water over low heat, stirring constantly. Allow to cool, but while still warm, mix 3 tablespoons sugar solution with lime juice in a blender. Add egg white and blend together. Mix in *pisco* and ice cubes, and blend until cubes are crushed. Pour into a glass and top with a drop of bitters. A foam layer will form on top.

*Pisco is a colorless brandy distilled from grapes. The Salaverrys recommend *pisco acholado,* which is blended from a mixture of grape cultures.

Cocktail de Algarrobina

Creamy cocktail made with pisco *and carob syrup.* Serves 4.

This recipe was provided by Teresa Bancallán de Castillo and Lizandro Castillo Salazar, owners of El Rincón del Pato. Their restaurant is in the department of Lambayeque and specializes in typical *criollo* cuisine.

6 OUNCES EVAPORATED MILK

6 OUNCES *PISCO**

2 EGG YOLKS

½ CUP WATER

8 ICE CUBES

PINCH NUTMEG

1½ TABLESPOONS CAROB SYRUP†

GROUND CINNAMON

Place milk, *pisco,* egg yolks, water and ice cubes in a blender and mix for 2–3 minutes. Add nutmeg and carob syrup and blend until well mixed. Serve in cocktail glasses and top with cinnamon.

Pisco is a colorless brandy distilled from grapes.

†Sweet syrup, *jarabe* (or *salsa) de algarrobina,* made from dried pods of the carob tree.

Chicha Morada

Nonalcoholic Andean drink made with purple corn. Serves many.

This traditional drink, popular throughout the year, is the beverage of choice in summer. Colored by purple corn that grows in the Andes mountains, it gives off a fantastic aroma as it cooks.

20 CUPS WATER

1 POUND DRIED PURPLE CORN ON THE COB (*MAÍZ MORADA*)

3 STICKS CINNAMON

PEEL OF ONE PINEAPPLE

2½ OUNCES DRIED CHERRIES (*GUINDAS,* OPTIONAL)

2 TEASPOONS WHOLE CLOVES

½ CUP FINELY DICED PINEAPPLE

1 CUP FINELY DICED, PEELED APPLE

1 CUP SUGAR

2 TABLESPOONS KEY LIME JUICE

In a large pot, bring water, corn, cinnamon sticks, pineapple peel, cherries and cloves to a boil. Boil for one hour. Strain liquid; discard corn, fruit and whole spices. Add sugar and lime juice. Add diced fruit when cool. Serve chilled.

APPETIZERS

Causa de Pulpa de Cangrejo

Layered cold mashed potato cake with fillings of avocado and crab meat. Serves 6. This recipe was provided by Adolfo Miguel Perret Bermúdez (shown on cover), chef and owner of the Punta Sal restaurant chain in Lima, which specializes in fish and seafood dishes. (See photo in color insert, first page, top right.)

1 3-INCH ROUND MOLD OR COOKIE CUTTER

3 POUNDS YELLOW POTATOES (YUKON GOLD, FOR EXAMPLE)

SALT AND PEPPER TO TASTE

⅔ CUP FINELY CHOPPED RED ONION

2 CLOVES GARLIC, MINCED

⅛ CUP VEGETABLE OIL

1 TEASPOON WATER

3 TABLESPOONS *AJÍ AMARILLO* PASTE*

JUICE OF 2 KEY LIMES

1 AVOCADO

Crab meat salad

7 OUNCES FRESH COOKED CRAB MEAT

½ CUP MAYONNAISE

SALT AND PEPPER TO TASTE

Dressing

4 TEASPOONS MAYONNAISE

2 TABLESPOONS PURPLE OLIVE PASTE

1 TEASPOON MUSTARD

½ TEASPOON MINCED GARLIC

Garnish

A FEW SPRIGS OF CILANTRO DIPPED IN OLIVE OIL

6 LETTUCE LEAVES

[Causa de Pulpa de Cangrejo, *continued*]

> 6 BLACK OLIVES
>
> 3 HARD-BOILED EGGS, QUARTERED
>
> 3½ OUNCES FARMER'S CHEESE (*QUESO FRESCO*), CUT IN SIX SLICES

Boil the potatoes in salted water, being careful that they don't split open. When the potatoes are soft and while still hot, peel and mash them. Season with salt and pepper to taste, and set aside.

Sauté onion and garlic in oil. To make a paste of the vegetables, place onion and garlic in a small blender with 1 teaspoon water, and blend until smooth. Add vegetable paste, chile-pepper paste and lime juice to the mashed potatoes. Mix well. Add vegetable oil to the potato mixture as needed to prevent it from sticking. Divide the potato mixture into six parts, one for each *causa*. Pat out one potato portion into a layer about ½-inch thick. Cut with the mold to form the three layers of the *causa,* leaving the mold in place on the last circle. Place thin slices of avocado on the potato layer inside the mold. Place another potato round over the avocado slices, sliding the mold up as necessary. Cover this potato layer with crab meat salad made by mixing cooked crab meat with mayonnaise, salt and pepper. Place the third potato layer on top of the crab meat and carefully remove the mold. Repeat until six *causas* are constructed.

To make the dressing, blend mayonnaise with olive paste, mustard and garlic, and spread a thin layer on top of each *causa*. Decorate with a few sprigs of cilantro. Serve on a lettuce leaf and garnish with an olive, two quarters of hard-boiled egg, and a slice of cheese.

*Despite the name (literally, yellow chile pepper), this Peruvian chile pepper is orange. *Ají amarillo* paste is available in many markets selling Latino foods, or see p. 70 for a recipe to make your own.

Ceviche de Pescado

Spicy marinated fish. Serves 4.

The recipe for this enormously popular national dish was provided by Cucho La Rosa, one of Peru's leading restaurateurs and chefs. La Rosa is Director of the culinary program for Cenfotur, a school that provides occupational training for the tourism industry. *Ceviche* traditionally is served on a bed of lettuce with a piece of sweet potato and a round of corn on the cob. (See photo in color insert, seventh page, top left.)

> 12 OUNCES VERY FRESH TILAPIA FILLETS, CUT INTO BITE-SIZE PIECES
>
> ½ MEDIUM RED ONION, THINLY SLICED INTO HALF RINGS
>
> 2 CHILE PEPPERS OF DIFFERENT COLOR, DESEEDED, DEVEINED AND
>
>   CUT INTO ROUNDS*

JUICE OF 7 KEY LIMES (SQUEEZED BY HAND)

¾ TEASPOON SALT, OR TO TASTE

ICE CUBES

Working rapidly, mix fish and onion in a bowl. Rinse with cold water and drain well. Add chile pepper, lime juice and salt, and mix well. Add a handful of ice cubes to be sure mixture is still chilled. Stir and quickly remove ice cubes so the juice is not diluted significantly. Serve and eat immediately.

*The preferred chile pepper for *ceviche* is the small Peruvian *ají limo,* an aromatic chile pepper that is available in several different colors. As this chile pepper is hard to find in the United States, jalapeño and serrano peppers may be substituted.

Papas a la Huancaina

Potatoes in the style of Huancayo. Serves 6–8.

The recipe for this specialty of the city of Huancayo in the department of Junín in south central Peru was provided by Javier and Jodie Castaneda. Javier is a native of Lima, Peru, who now resides with his wife and family in the United States. The dish is a family favorite.

2 TEASPOONS ACHIOTE (ANNATTO) SEEDS

¼ CUP VEGETABLE OIL

15 OUNCES FARMER'S CHEESE*

2 *AJÍES AMARILLOS,* DESEEDED, DEVEINED AND SLICED LENGTHWISE;

    SET ASIDE 4–6 SLICES FOR GARNISH†

1 12-OUNCE CAN EVAPORATED MILK

6–8 SALTINE CRACKERS

SALT AND PEPPER TO TASTE

LETTUCE LEAVES

4–6 MEDIUM YELLOW OR WHITE POTATOES, BOILED (FIRM) AND PEELED

3–4 HARD-BOILED EGGS, SLICED

BLACK OLIVES, PITTED AND SLICED

1 EAR BOILED CORN, CUT INTO 2-INCH ROUNDS

Fry annatto seeds in oil until the oil becomes reddish. Set aside and cool. Remove seeds and residue. In a blender, emulsify cheese, reddened oil and peppers. Add evaporated milk and crackers, and continue blending to make a pourable cream. Add salt and pepper to taste.

To serve, cover a platter with lettuce leaves. Slice boiled potatoes lengthwise and arrange on lettuce, cut sides up. Pour sauce over potatoes and lettuce. Garnish with eggs, olives, pepper slices and corn.

[Papas a la Huacaina, *continued*]
*Queso fresco, a non-melting cheese, is recommended.
†Despite the name (yellow chile pepper), this Peruvian chile pepper is orange.

SALAD

Ensalada Belga de Endibia y Queso Roquefort

Belgian endive and Roquefort salad. Serves 4.

This recipe was provided by Jorge (Coque) Luis Ossio Guiulfo, chef/owner of La Bombonniere in the San Isidro neighborhood of Lima and the Inka Grill in Cuzco. Coque is a member of Peru's well-known family of restaurateurs and caterers headed by his mother, Marisa Guiulfo Zender.

Dijon vinaigrette

⅓ CUP OLIVE OIL

1½ TABLESPOONS WHITE WINE VINEGAR

1 TABLESPOON DIJON MUSTARD

1 CLOVE GARLIC, MINCED

SALT AND PEPPER TO TASTE

Salad

20 WHOLE BELGIAN ENDIVE LEAVES

2 TOMATOES, DESEEDED AND FINELY CHOPPED

4 CUPS TORN BELGIAN ENDIVE LEAVES

2 OUNCES DIJON VINAIGRETTE

Cream sauce

3 OUNCES ROQUEFORT CHEESE

½ CUP SOUR CREAM

1 TABLESPOON MILK

SALT TO TASTE

Garnish

¼ CUP CHOPPED CANDIED WALNUTS*

FRESH CHIVES

Whisk vinaigrette ingredients together. Arrange five whole endive leaves on each plate like the points of a star. Combine tomatoes, torn endive and 2 tablespoons vinaigrette, or to taste. Arrange in the center of each plate. Blend cheese, sour cream, milk and salt to form a sauce, and drizzle over tomato-endive mixture. Serve topped with candied walnuts and long pieces of chives.

*Available in the nuts and dried fruits section of most grocery stores.

SOUPS/CHOWDERS

Crema de Zapallo Loche Aromatizado de Curry con Conchas

Curry-flavored cream of squash soup with scallops. Serves 8.

Michael Raas, corporate executive chef of the Peruvian hotels and trains owned by Orient Express, provided the recipe for this delicious dish. It is served on the luxurious Hiram Bingham train between Cuzco and Machu Picchu Pueblo (formerly called Aguas Calientes) at the base of Machu Picchu.

2 POUNDS BUTTERNUT SQUASH*

8 PIECES STAR ANISE

2 STICKS CINNAMON

10 CLOVES GARLIC, MINCED

4¼ POUNDS RED ONIONS, CUT INTO THICK STRIPS

½ CUP VEGETABLE OIL

2 POUNDS (VERY RIPE) TOMATOES, DESEEDED AND CUT INTO THICK STRIPS

1 TABLESPOON CHOPPED CILANTRO

2 CUPS PERUVIAN CORN BEER, *CHICHA DE JORA*†

2 TEASPOONS *AJÍ AMARILLO* PASTE††

4 CUPS CHICKEN BROTH

1½ TEASPOONS *MASAMAN* CURRY PASTE†††

½ CUP WHIPPING CREAM

24 SCALLOPS

A FEW DROPS OF LEMON JUICE

SALT AND WHITE PEPPER TO TASTE

3 TABLESPOONS BUTTER

2 CLOVES GARLIC, MINCED

1 TEASPOON CHOPPED PARSLEY

10 SPRIGS CILANTRO FOR DECORATION

Cut the squash in half, remove seeds and fibrous flesh lining the seed cavity, and place squash hollow-side up in a baking dish. Put anise and cinnamon in the hollows.

[Crema de Zapallo Loche Aromatizado de Curry con Conchas, *continued*]
Add about ½ inch of water to the pan. Bake at 375°F until soft, about 1½ hours.
Discard the spices. Scoop out the flesh and beat until fluffy. Press through a sieve to
remove any remaining fibers. In a large frying pan, sauté garlic and onion in oil over
medium-high heat until onions are soft. Stir in tomatoes and cilantro, and fry
another 10 minutes. In a large saucepan, mix vegetables with the *chicha de jora,*
chile-pepper paste and chicken broth. Cook and reduce volume over moderate-high
heat for about 25 minutes, stirring frequently. Strain, pressing down on vegetables
to extract remaining liquid. Let softer vegetables pass through the sieve; discard
remaining vegetables. Add squash and curry paste, and blend well. This squash
mixture can be made ahead and frozen. Whip cream and fold in. Season scallops
with a few drops of lemon juice, salt and white pepper to taste. Grill rapidly in
butter, garlic and parsley. Place three scallops in the center of each soup bowl, and
cover with squash soup. Garnish with a sprig of cilantro.
*Butternut squash is a substitute for the Peruvian squash *zapallo loche.*
†White wine is a reasonable substitute for *chicha de jora* in this recipe.
††*Ají amarillo* paste is available in many Latino markets, or see p. 70 for a recipe to
make your own.
†††Available at Asian, Indian and specialty food markets.

Cauche de Camarones

Peruvian-style fondue with shrimp and yellow potatoes. Serves 4.

This award-winning recipe was provided by chef Alcario Callyahua at Sol de Mayo,
the oldest *picantería* in Arequipa. *Cauche de camarones* was created by Celmira
Cerpa, daughter of the restaurant's founder and current owner of the restaurant,
who invented many of the dishes served at the restaurant. (See photo in color insert,
second page, top left)

8 OUNCES SMALL YELLOW POTATOES (YUKON GOLD, FOR EXAMPLE)

⅔ CUP CHOPPED ONION

3½ TABLESPOONS BUTTER

8 OUNCES TOMATO SAUCE

1 TABLESPOON VEGETABLE OIL

SALT TO TASTE

8 OUNCES CLEANED SHRIMP

1 POUND MELTING CHEESE, SHREDDED*

¾ CUP EVAPORATED MILK

¼ TEASPOON SALT

2 TEASPOONS COARSELY CHOPPED FLAT-LEAF PARSLEY

Peel and boil potatoes. Cut in half when cooked, and set aside. Sauté onion in butter until limp. Add tomato sauce and cook over medium heat until the mixture thickens and the bottom of the pan can be seen when a spoon is drawn across it. Put oil and salt in a frying pan and fry shrimp. Set aside. Add cheese, evaporated milk and salt to the tomato mixture. Bring to a boil and continue cooking until cheese is completely melted, stirring frequently. Add potatoes and shrimp. Serve hot in individual bowls, garnished with parsley.

*Some melting cheeses available at many Latino and specialty food markets are *queso quesadilla* and *queso asadero*. Although commonly found at these markets, *queso fresco* is not a melting cheese.

Chupe de Pallares Verdes

Lima bean chowder. Serves 6.

This recipe was provided by Cristel Carrasco Gonzales, owner of El Catador Restaurant and Winery in the department of Ica.

6 CLOVES GARLIC, MINCED

2 TABLESPOONS VEGETABLE OIL

12 CUPS WATER

1 POUND FROZEN LIMA BEANS

2 EARS OF CORN, CUT CROSSWISE INTO 1-INCH ROUNDS

4 YELLOW POTATOES (YUKON GOLD, FOR EXAMPLE), PEELED AND CUBED

1 TEASPOON SALT, OR TO TASTE

¼ TEASPOON PEPPER

¾ POUND VERMICELLI, BROKEN INTO 2–3-INCH PIECES

1 CUP EVAPORATED MILK

2 TABLESPOONS ASIAN DRIED SHRIMP

1 *AJÍ AMARILLO,* CUT INTO STRIPS*

1 TABLESPOON DRIED OREGANO

6 EGGS, UNBEATEN

¼ POUND *QUESO FRESCO,* CUT INTO SMALL CUBES†

Sauté garlic in oil until golden. Add water and bring to a boil. Add frozen lima beans, corn, potatoes, salt and pepper. Return to a boil for 5 minutes. Add vermicelli and continue boiling for 10 minutes. Add milk, shrimp, chile pepper and

[Chupe de Pallares Verdes, *continued*]
oregano, and cook for about 5 minutes longer. Slowly add eggs and stir until cooked, about 10 minutes. Eggs will become dispersed as threads. Distribute cheese cubes in soup bowls and ladle stew on top.

*Despite the name (yellow chile pepper), this Peruvian chile pepper is orange.

†*Queso fresco* is a non-melting cheese. Do not substitute melting cheeses such as *queso asadero* and *queso quesadilla*.

Main Dishes

Canilla de Cordero con Puré de Papa y Salsa de Cabernet Shiraz al Curry Andino

Lamb shanks with puréed potato in a wine and Andean curry sauce. Serves 4.

This recipe, provided by Rafael Piqueras, chef at the Sonesta Posadas del Inca restaurant in Lima, originally called for *carillera de cerdo,* or pork jowls. As pork jowls are not readily available everywhere, the chef suggested lamb shanks as a substitute. (See photo in color insert, sixth page, top right.)

Andean curry

1 WHOLE *AJÍ PANCA**

¼ TEASPOON PINK PEPPERCORNS, GROUND

⅛ TEASPOON LIME ZEST

⅛ TEASPOON CUMIN

⅛ TEASPOON DRIED OR ¾ TEASPOON FROZEN *HUACATAY*†

⅛ TEASPOON DRIED OR ¾ TEASPOON FRESH CHOPPED SPEARMINT

½ TEASPOON MINCED JALAPEÑO OR SERRANO CHILE PEPPER

¼ TEASPOON MINCED ONION

⅛ TEASPOON MINCED GARLIC

½ TEASPOON ACHIOTE OIL††

8 LAMB SHANKS, ABOUT 1 INCH THICK

SALT AND PEPPER TO TASTE

¼ CUP OLIVE OIL

1 RED ONION, COARSELY CHOPPED

3 STALKS CELERY, COARSELY CHOPPED

2 CARROTS, COARSELY CHOPPED

3–4 OUNCES SLICED MUSHROOMS

2 CUPS CABERNET SHIRAZ WINE

4 CUPS CHICKEN BROTH

1 BOUQUET GARNI OF 1 SPRIG EACH OF FRESH SPEARMINT AND ROSEMARY

Potato purée

6 YELLOW POTATOES (YUKON GOLD, FOR EXAMPLE)

1 CUP HEAVY CREAM, WARMED

1 STICK BUTTER

1 CUP GRATED PARMESAN CHEESE

SALT AND PEPPER TO TASTE

To make the curry, cut open the dried chile pepper and discard the seeds and veins. Fry in a little oil for about 1 minute over medium heat, turning once or twice, being careful not to burn the pepper. Be sure to ventilate well while frying to remove pungent pepper fumes. Transfer the pepper from the frying pan to a small pan of boiling water. Remove from heat and use a heavy object to keep the pepper submerged for 1 hour. Then remove the pepper from the water, pat dry with paper towels and mash it to a paste with a mortar and pestle. Mix in ground pink pepper, lime zest, cumin, *huacatay,* spearmint, green chile pepper, onion, garlic and achiote oil. Set aside.

Season shanks with salt and pepper. Fry in olive oil until golden brown on both sides. Remove from pan and set aside. Add onion, celery, carrots and mushrooms to frying pan and sauté until golden. Put meat and wine in a casserole dish or Dutch oven that also can be used on the stovetop. Bring to a boil. Let boil for 1 minute, then add broth, sautéed vegetables and bouquet garni. Cover and cook in a 350°F oven until meat is tender, approximately 2 hours. While meat is in the oven, cook and mash potatoes. When smooth, add warmed cream and mix well. Add butter, cheese, salt and pepper and purée until potatoes are very creamy. Set aside and keep warm.

Remove meat from oven and set aside. Strain juices and discard vegetables. Over medium-high heat, reduce volume of juices by half. Add 1 teaspoon of the curry and blend well. Add meat and continue to reduce juices until about 1 cup of juice remains. To serve, arrange some potato purée on a plate. Top with a lamb shank and drizzle sauce over meat and potato. Decorate with a sprig of fresh rosemary.

*Ají panca is the dried form of the chile pepper known as *ají colorado.*

†A pungent herb. In the United States it is available frozen and dried at many Latino and specialty food markets.

††Produced by frying achiote (annatto) seeds in oil; used as a flavorant and coloring agent.

Lenguado al Vapor en Salsa de Maracuyá

Steamed sole in passion fruit sauce. Serves 2.

This recipe was provided by Santiago Solari Morgan, chef and owner of Ñaylamp in the Barranco neighborhood of Lima.

6 TABLESPOONS WHITE WINE

½ TEASPOON SUGAR

6 TABLESPOONS FRESH PASSION FRUIT JUICE, STRAINED*

8 OUNCES *CREMA DE LECHE*†

⅛ TEASPOON SALT

1 SOLE FILLET (6–8 OUNCES)

SALT TO TASTE

BLACK SESAME OIL

1 CLOVE GARLIC, MINCED

2 OUNCES RAW SHRIMP, DEVEINED

4 OUNCES RICE, COOKED

In a small frying pan over medium heat, reduce wine and sugar to one-third its volume. Mixture will become golden brown and remain clear; do not let it caramelize. Add passion fruit juice, *crema de leche* and salt, and reduce sauce until it thickens. Season fish with salt, brush with sesame oil and spread garlic uniformly on top. Place fish in a basket, preferably made of bamboo, and steam over boiling water for 4 minutes. Add shrimp to the basket and steam for 3 minutes more. Serve fish with sauce. Top with shrimp, and serve with rice on the side.
*Boxed or bottled juice can be substituted.
†Also called *crema fresca*. Available at many Latino grocery stores.

Tamalitos Verdes

Savory corn tamales with spinach. Makes 12 tamales.

This recipe was provided by Teresa Bancallán de Castillo and Lizandro Castillo Salazar, owners of El Rincón del Pato. This restaurant in Lambayeque, a city near Chiclayo in the department of Lambayeque, specializes in typical *criollo* cuisine. (See color insert for photo, fourth page, middle left.)

1 PACKAGE DRIED CORNHUSKS

1 POUND FRESH SPINACH, STEMS REMOVED

1 CUP BUTTERNUT SQUASH, GRATED AND PACKED*

½ RED BELL PEPPER, DESEEDED, DEVEINED AND CUT IN LARGE PIECES

2 *AJÍES AMARILLOS,* DESEEDED AND DEVEINED†

3 SCALLIONS, CUT IN LARGE PIECES

2 CLOVES GARLIC

½ CUP EVAPORATED MILK

2½ TEASPOONS SALT

¼ TEASPOON PEPPER

12 OUNCES CORN FLOUR (*HARINA DE MAÍZ*), NOT INSTANT

3 TABLESPOONS LARD

To prepare cornhusks, bring water to a boil in a large pan. Turn off burner and submerge husks in water to soften. To make the tamales, grind spinach, squash, peppers, scallions and garlic to a paste in a food processor. Add milk, salt and pepper, and blend well. Remove mixture to a large bowl and add flour. When completely mixed, blend in lard. Divide mixture into 12 portions and pat each portion into an oblong shape, about 4 inches long. To assemble the tamales, lay two cornhusks together, overlapping them by about 2 inches at their wider ends. Lay a third husk over them, crosswise, in the middle. Lay a tamale filling on the third husk, positioning it lengthwise in relation to the two husks at the bottom. Roll the third husk around the filling. Then fold the other husks, one at a time, around the filling, and tie the "package" securely with kitchen twine. Submerge the tamales in boiling water, reduce the heat and simmer for 30 minutes. Serve with thinly sliced lemon and *salsa criolla* (see recipe, p. 70).

*Butternut squash is a substitute for the Peruvian squash *zapallo loche*.

†Despite the name (yellow chile pepper), this Peruvian chile pepper is orange.

Pescado Sudado

Steamed fish. Serves 2.

The recipe for this simple, but delicious fish dish was contributed by Ana Debert de Kesch, chef and owner of the Club Colonial restaurant in Huanchaco, a fishing community near Trujillo in the department of La Libertad. (See photo in color insert, seventh page, bottom.)

½ POUND YUCA, PEELED

1 TABLESPOON *AJÍ PANCA* PASTE, OR TO TASTE*

3 TILAPIA FILLETS†

JUICE OF 3 KEY LIMES, FRESHLY SQUEEZED

½ TEASPOON SALT, OR TO TASTE

⅛ TEASPOON PEPPER, OR TO TASTE

8 CLOVES GARLIC, MINCED

2 LARGE RED ONIONS, CUT INTO LARGE CHUNKS

[Pescado Sudado, *continued*]

> 2 TABLESPOONS VEGETABLE OIL
>
> 4 MEDIUM TOMATOES, CUT IN WEDGES
>
> 1 *AJÍ AMARILLO,* DESEEDED, DEVEINED AND CUT INTO
>
>   NARROW STRIPS††
>
> 2 TABLESPOONS CILANTRO LEAVES

Cut yuca in 2-inch lengths. Cut the lengths in quarters vertically, and remove the thin, stringy core. Boil in salted water for about 10 minutes. Add ½ cup cold water to pan and boil another 5 minutes or until soft and somewhat translucent. Drain, set aside and keep warm. Briefly marinate fish in lime juice, salt and pepper. In a Dutch oven, sauté garlic and onions in oil. While onions are still crunchy, stir in *ají panca* paste. Top with tomatoes and strips of pepper. Place fish over this bed of vegetables and pour marinade over the top. Sprinkle cilantro over all, cover and steam for 7 minutes. Serve with yuca.

*The original recipe calls for Sybarita, a commercial mixture of powdered *ají panca* (a dried chile pepper) and other spices, which is used to flavor and color foods. It is not widely available in the United States. A simple paste of *ají panca* is available in many markets carrying Latino foods, or see p. 70 for a recipe to make your own.

†Any flat white fish (such as sole) may be substituted.

††Despite its name (yellow chile pepper), this Peruvian chile pepper is orange.

Lomo Atún en Costar de Hierbas Peruanas, sobre Pastel de Choclo

Herb-coated tuna fillet atop a corn cake. Serves 4.

This recipe was provided by Marilú Madueño, chef at the Restaurant Huaca Pucllana in the Miraflores neighborhood of Lima. The restaurant overlooks the ruins of a pre-colonial adobe pyramid. (See photo in color insert, first page, top left.)

> *Tomato preserve*
>
> 4 FIRM RIPE TOMATOES, SKINNED, QUARTERED AND DESEEDED*
>
> 1 TABLESPOON OLIVE OIL
>
> 1 TABLESPOON BALSAMIC VINEGAR
>
> 1 TABLESPOON SUGAR
>
> SALT AND PEPPER TO TASTE
>
> *Caper sauce*
>
> 2 TABLESPOONS OLIVE OIL
>
> 3 TABLESPOONS FINELY CHOPPED ONION

3 TABLESPOONS DICED BELL PEPPER

3 TABLESPOONS FINELY CHOPPED HABANERO PEPPERS†

3 TABLESPOONS CAPERS

1 TOMATO, DESEEDED AND FINELY CHOPPED

5 ARÚGULA LEAVES, CUT IN SMALL PIECES

1 TABLESPOON WHITE VINEGAR

SALT AND PEPPER TO TASTE

Corn cake

3 CUPS FRESH CORN KERNELS, REMOVED FROM THE COB (ABOUT FIVE EARS)

½ CUP MILK

1 MEDIUM ONION, FINELY CHOPPED

1 CLOVE GARLIC, MINCED

1 TABLESPOON VEGETABLE OIL

¼ TEASPOON SALT, OR TO TASTE

⅛ TEASPOON PEPPER

3 TABLESPOONS CORNMEAL

2 EGGS

Fish fillets

4 TUNA FILLETS, 7 OUNCES EACH

4 TABLESPOONS BREAD CRUMBS

1 TABLESPOON FINELY CHOPPED CILANTRO

1 TABLESPOON FRESH OR FROZEN FINELY CHOPPED *HUACATAY* ††

1 TABLESPOON FINELY CHOPPED PARSLEY

1 TABLESPOON FINELY CHOPPED MINT

OLIVE OIL FOR FRYING

To make the tomato preserve, put tomatoes in a small baking dish with olive oil, vinegar, sugar, salt and pepper. Bake at 350°F for about 1 hour, stirring occasionally. Tomatoes will be soft but intact.

For the caper sauce, cook olive oil, onion, bell pepper, habanero chile pepper and capers in a small pan over low heat for a few minutes. Then add tomato and arúgula. Season with vinegar, salt and pepper.

To make the corn cake, purée corn with milk in a blender at high speed for about 3 minutes. Strain mixture well, pressing it with the back of a spoon to extract as much liquid as possible. Discard hulls. Sauté onion and garlic in oil in a frying pan. Add corn mixture and cook over medium-high heat until thick, about 2–3 minutes. Remove from heat. Add salt, pepper, cornmeal and well-beaten eggs, and transfer to

[Lomo Atún en Costar de Hierbas Peruanas, sobre Pastel de Choclo, *continued*]
a greased 8" × 8" baking dish. Bake at 350°F until cake is firm and golden on top,
about 1 hour. Allow the cake to cool, then cut into 4 pieces. Cake should be soft
but not mushy.

To prepare the fish, mix herbs with bread crumbs. Coat the fish in olive oil and
dredge in herb and bread-crumb mixture. Put a little olive oil in a frying pan, and
fry fish on both sides until it is golden on the outside but still red within.

To serve, cut each tuna fillet diagonally to form two triangles. Stand both halves on
end, side-by-side, with the cut edges facing in opposite directions. Trim bottom
edges if necessary to make pieces stand upright. Top with a sprig of parsley.
Surround fish-topped corn cake with some tomato preserves, and drizzle with caper
sauce.

*Dip whole tomatoes in boiling water for 10–15 seconds to aid in removing skin.

†To reduce the heat of the peppers, cut them in half, remove seeds and veins, and
boil a few minutes. Drain and repeat.

††A pungent herb used fresh. In the United States, it is available frozen and dried
at certain Latino and specialty food markets. May substitute ½ teaspoon dried
huacatay in this recipe.

Cabrito a la Norteña con Fríjol Redondo

*Suckling goat in the northern style: marinated in corn beer and vinegar, and served
with beans.* Serves 8.

This recipe was provided by Gloria Yaipen Chafloque, chef and mother of César
Flores, owner of Restaurant La Perla de las Flores in Chiclayo, in the department of
Lambayeque. (See photo in color insert, third page, top left.)

> *Beans*
>
> 1 CUP CANARY BEANS*
>
> 2 TABLESPOONS EVAPORATED MILK
>
> 1 CUP COOKING BROTH
>
> 2 CLOVES GARLIC, MINCED
>
> 1 TABLESPOON FINELY CHOPPED RED ONION
>
> 1 TEASPOON *AJÍ AMARILLO* PASTE†
>
> ½ TEASPOON SALT
>
> PEPPER TO TASTE
>
> 1 TEASPOON VEGETABLE OIL
>
> *Meat*
>
> 4 POUNDS SUCKLING GOAT (CAN SUBSTITUTE LAMB)
>
> SALT AND PEPPER TO TASTE

2 TABLESPOONS RED WINE VINEGAR

½ CUP PERUVIAN CORN BEER, *CHICHA DE JORA*††

1 CUP (DENSELY PACKED) CILANTRO LEAVES

1½ CUPS DICED BUTTERNUT SQUASH†††

¾ CUP DICED CARROTS

¾ CUP WATER

2 TABLESPOONS MINCED GARLIC

¼ CUP VEGETABLE OIL

1–2 TEASPOONS *AJÍ AMARILLO* PASTE†

½ CUP CHOPPED SCALLIONS

3–4 MEDIUM TOMATOES, DESEEDED AND DICED

½ TEASPOON CUMIN

SALT AND PEPPER TO TASTE

1 TOMATO, DESEEDED AND CUT INTO LARGE WEDGES

1 *AJÍ AMARILLO,* DESEEDED, DEVEINED AND

    CUT INTO LARGE PIECES†

6 CUPS RICE, COOKED

To prepare beans, cover with water and soak overnight. The next day, rub beans together to remove loose skins, and rinse to flush the skins away. Boil beans in fresh, salted water until soft, about 1½ hour. Drain beans and transfer to a saucepan. Reserve cooking broth. In a blender, purée ⅓ of the cooked beans (about ½ cup) in the evaporated milk and cooking broth. Add mixture to drained beans. Sauté garlic, onion, *ají amarillo* paste, salt and pepper in oil and add to bean mixture. Set aside. Season meat with salt and pepper. Add vinegar and *chicha de jora,* and marinate meat while preparing vegetables. Place cilantro, squash, carrots and water in a blender, and grind into a paste.

In a large pot, sauté garlic in oil until light brown. Blend in chile paste. Add meat, reserving marinade, and brown evenly over high heat for 3 minutes. Add marinade, scallions, tomatoes, paste of cilantro, squash and carrots, cumin and salt to taste. Cook for 10 minutes without a cover, then cover and cook for another 20 minutes. Add 1 cup water and continue to cook, uncovered, until meat is tender and sauce is thick and "dry." If sauce gets too dry before meat is tender, add more water and cook longer, again reducing the sauce until dry. Add tomato wedges and yellow chile-pepper pieces, cover and cook 5 minutes more.

Serve on a bed of rice, decorated with some pieces of tomato and chile pepper. On the side, place some beans and top them with a drizzle of meat sauce.

*Frijol canario or *frijol peruano,* a pale-yellow bean native to Peru. Available at Latino grocery stores.

[Cabrito a la Norteña con Fríjol Redondo, *continued*]

†Despite the name (literally, yellow chile pepper), this Peruvian chile pepper is orange. *Ají amarillo* paste is available in many markets carrying Latino foods, or see p. 70 for a recipe to make your own.

††Light beer is a reasonable substitute for *chicha de jora* in this recipe.

†††Butternut squash is a substitute for the Peruvian squash *zapallo loche*.

Tacu Tacu de Pallares en Salsa de Camarones

Bean and rice patty served with shrimp sauce. Serves 4.

The recipe for this popular dish, which typically is made with leftover beans and rice, was provided by Luis Felipe Arizola Gadea, chef and owner of A Puerta Cerrada restaurant in Barranco, Lima, which features traditional Peruvian foods. (See photo in color insert, third page, middle.)

½ POUND DRIED CANARY BEANS*

¼ POUND FAT BACK OR SALT PORK, DICED

2 TABLESPOONS VEGETABLE OIL

1 MEDIUM ONION, FINELY CHOPPED

1 LARGE CLOVE GARLIC, MINCED

3 TABLESPOONS *AJÍ AMARILLO* PASTE†

2 TEASPOONS DRIED OREGANO

¼ POUND RICE, COOKED

SALT AND PEPPER TO TASTE

Sauce

2 TABLESPOONS BUTTER

2 TABLESPOONS FLOUR

¾ CUP WHITE WINE

1 TEASPOON PAPRIKA

SALT AND PEPPER TO TASTE

8 OUNCES SHRIMP, COOKED

Cover beans with water and soak overnight. Rub together to remove loose skins and rinse to flush the skins away. In a large pot, cover beans and fat back with water, and boil until beans are soft, about 1½ hours. Drain and cool. In a food processor, grind the bean and fat-back mixture into a coarse purée. Set aside. Heat oil in a large frying pan over medium heat. Add onion and garlic, and sauté until golden, about 5 minutes. Add *ají amarillo* paste and oregano, and cook a few minutes more. Blend in bean mixture and rice, mixing well. Add salt and pepper to taste. Flatten mixture in pan and increase heat to high. As the *tacu tacu* becomes golden on the bottom, tip the pan away from you, letting the *tacu tacu* slide to the lower side of the pan. Shake the pan back and forth, and use a slight upward jerk to cause the mixture to fold onto itself. After several flips the *tacu tacu* forms a rough cylinder with pointed ends. Any small cracks that develop when it is flipped will seal again in the next few flips. Continue motion until the *tacu tacu* is nicely browned all over. Remove the *tacu tacu* to an oval serving platter and set aside.

To make the sauce, melt butter in a small saucepan over low heat. Add flour and whisk until smooth. Mix in wine and continue cooking on low heat until sauce thickens, stirring continuously. Add paprika, salt and pepper to taste, and shrimp, continuing to cook and stir until shrimp are heated through. Create a depression in the surface of the *tacu tacu* on the platter, then spoon shrimp and some of the sauce into the depression and on the serving platter.

*Fríjol canario or *fríjol peruano,* a pale-yellow bean native to Peru. Available at Latino grocery stores.

†Despite the name (yellow chile pepper), this Peruvian chile pepper is orange. *Ají amarillo* paste is available in many markets carrying Latino foods, or see p. 70 for a recipe to make your own.

Huatia Sulcana

Slow-cooked beef with fresh aromatic herbs. Serves 8.

Huatia was originally cooked in-ground on hot stones, but is now typically stewed in the oven in a clay pot. The recipe for this dish was provided by Flavio Solórzano Alvarez, executive chef at El Señorío de Sulca. This restaurant in the Miraflores district of Lima specializes in traditional Peruvian cuisine. (See cover photo.)

> *Chile-pepper seasoning*

2 TABLESPOONS *AJÍ PANCA* PASTE*

1 TABLESPOON MINCED GARLIC

1 TEASPOON BLACK PEPPER

1 TEASPOON TOASTED AND GROUND CUMIN

½ CUP VINEGAR

½ CUP VEGETABLE OIL

> *Herb mixture*

7 OUNCES FRESH MINT SPRIGS

2 OUNCES FRESH OREGANO SPRIGS

2 OUNCES FRESH ROSEMARY SPRIGS

2 OUNCES FRESH *HUACATAY* SPRIGS†

2 OUNCES FRESH CILANTRO SPRIGS

[Huatia Sulcana, *continued*]

> 2 OUNCES FRESH THYME SPRIGS
>
> 3½ POUNDS BONELESS CHUCK ROAST, CUT INTO 8 PIECES
>
> 2 MEDIUM ONIONS, CUT IN LARGE PIECES
>
> 2 *AJÍES AMARILLOS,* DESEEDED, DEVEINED AND
>
>   CUT INTO LARGE PIECES††
>
> 8 MEDIUM SWEET POTATOES (OF UNIFORM OVAL SHAPE)

To make *ají panca* paste, see recipe, p. 70. In a blender, combine *ají panca* paste, garlic, pepper, cumin, vinegar and oil. In an oven-proof casserole, layer ingredients in thirds as follows: herbs, chile-pepper seasoning, meat, onions and pieces of *ají amarillo*. Cover casserole with a tight-fitting lid and bake at 350°F until meat is done, about 2–3 hours. Meanwhile, peel sweet potatoes and bake in a covered casserole for 1 hour at 350°F, or until soft. Rotate potatoes once during baking. Serve meat in a soup bowl, topped with cooking juices and some of the onion and *ají amarillo*. Garnish with a sprig of fresh rosemary. Slice sweet potatoes in half and serve cut-side up alongside meat.

*The recipe calls for a paste of the finger-shaped *ají colorado* (*Capsicum chinense*), but it is more readily available in its dried form, *ají panca*.

†A pungent herb. In the United States, *huacatay* is available frozen or dried at some Latino and specialty food markets. May substitute 1 tablespoon frozen or ½ teaspoon dried *huacatay*.

††Despite the name (yellow chile pepper), this Peruvian chile pepper is orange.

Quinotto

Mixture of quinoa and vegetables. Serves 6.

This recipe was provided by Denise Koechlin, co-owner of the Machu Picchu Pueblo Hotel in Machu Picchu Pueblo (formerly called Aguas Calientes). *Quinotto* is a play on the word "risotto," substituting quinoa for rice (although the cooking process is not the same as that used to make a risotto). Quinoa is a protein-rich seed that becomes translucent when cooked, except for the external germ, which is opaque.

> 1 MEDIUM TOMATO, DESEEDED AND FINELY CHOPPED
>
> 1 TABLESPOON OLIVE OIL
>
> ¼ TEASPOON BASIL
>
> 1 CLOVE GARLIC, MINCED
>
> ¼ CUP PEAS

¼ CUP DICED CARROTS

4 STRIPS BACON

1 MEDIUM ONION, FINELY CHOPPED

¼ CUP COARSELY CHOPPED MUSHROOMS

¼ TEASPOON PAPRIKA

½ TABLESPOON BACON FAT

2¼ CUPS WATER

1⅛ CUP QUINOA

1 CUP WHITE WINE

⅔ CUP HEAVY CREAM

1 TEASPOON SALT, OR TO TASTE

PEPPER TO TASTE

Marinate tomato in frying pan with olive oil, basil and garlic. Boil or steam peas and carrots until done. Fry bacon, drain and crumble into small pieces. Add crumbled bacon, onion, mushrooms, paprika and bacon fat to tomato mixture, and pan fry until onions are translucent. Rinse quinoa several times in cold water until water runs clear. Bring water to a boil and add quinoa. Cover and cook over medium heat for 12–15 minutes, or until water level is below the level of the quinoa. Do not let water boil off completely. Drain. Add quinoa, peas, carrots, wine, cream, salt and pepper to tomato mixture in frying pan, and stir over medium heat for 5 minutes.

Lomo en Salsa de Sauco con Tarta de Quinua

Beef fillet with elderberry sauce served with a quinoa tart. Serves 2.
This recipe was provided by Denise Koechlin, co-owner with her husband, Jose, of the Machu Picchu Pueblo Hotel in Machu Picchu Pueblo (formerly called Aguas Calientes). The Koechlins have owned the hotel since 1991 and also own Reserva Amazonical Lodge in Puerto Maldonado. (See photo in color insert, last page, top.)

Elderberry sauce

1 SLICE BACON

2 TABLESPOONS ELDERBERRY SYRUP*

2 TABLESPOONS WORCESTERSHIRE SAUCE

2 TABLESPOONS CAROB SYRUP†

2 TABLESPOONS COGNAC

Quinoa pancakes

¼ CUP QUINOA

[Lomo en Salsa de Sauco con Tarta de Quinua, *continued*]

¾ CUP WATER

2 EGGS, BEATEN

⅓ CUP FLOUR

¼ TEASPOON SALT

PEPPER TO TASTE

Tart filling and garnish

½ TEASPOON CUMIN

2 TEASPOONS WHITE WINE

2 TEASPOONS LEMON JUICE

SALT AND PEPPER TO TASTE

½ CUP WHIPPING CREAM AT ROOM TEMPERATURE

½ CUP FRESH SPINACH LEAVES

WHOLE CHIVES

Onion garnish

½ CUP RED ONIONS, SLICED

½ CUP RED WINE

2 7-OUNCE BEEF FILLETS

To make elderberry sauce, fry bacon in a small frying pan until crisp. Break into small pieces with a spoon. Discard most of the fat. Add the rest of the sauce ingredients and cook over medium heat for about 30 seconds. To make the quinoa tart, rinse quinoa briefly in cold water until the water runs clear. Drain. In a small, tightly covered saucepan, cook quinoa in ¾ cup water for 12 minutes. Begin with medium heat; reduce to a simmer when it boils. After 12 minutes, remove from heat and allow to stand, covered, for 15 minutes while making the spinach filling. Add cumin, wine, lemon juice, salt and pepper to room-temperature cream, and stir well. Cream "sours" and thickens on addition of lemon. Steam spinach 1–2 minutes to soften. Add to cream sauce.

To make quinoa pancakes, fluff quinoa, add egg and mix well. Add flour, salt and pepper. On a heated, oiled griddle, ladle mixture to form 6 pancakes about 2½–3 inches in diameter. Lightly brown pancakes on each side. To construct the tart, stack three pancakes, putting some spinach cream between them. Spear top pancake in each stack with some whole chives. Fry onions in wine until soft. Broil steak to taste. Serve butterflied, surrounded by some onion garnish, elderberry sauce and a quinoa tart.

*Can substitute fresh elderberries.

†A sweet syrup, *jarabe* (or *salsa*) *de algarrobina,* made from the dried pods of the carob tree.

Espesado de Vacuno

Beef ribs in a thick sauce with yuca and squash. Serves 3–4.

This recipe was contributed by Alberto Solis Serrepe, owner of Fiesta Restaurant Gourmet in Lambayeque, a small city near Chiclayo. The Serrape family owns a chain of Fiesta Restaurants in Peru and Chile.

1 POUND YUCA

2 CUPS FRESH CORN (ABOUT 3 EARS), CUT FROM THE COB

1 CUP FRESH CILANTRO LEAVES, PACKED

1–3 TABLESPOONS WATER

1½ POUNDS BEEF SHORT RIBS (HAVE BUTCHER CUT THEM IN HALF)

½ TEASPOON SALT

¼ TEASPOON PEPPER

3½ OUNCES GRATED BUTTERNUT SQUASH*

1 SCALLION, CUT LENGTHWISE INTO STRIPS

1 SMALL RED BELL PEPPER, SEEDED AND CUT INTO VERTICAL STRIPS

2 CUPS COOKED RICE, COLORED WITH ⅛ TEASPOON TURMERIC

CEVICHE DE PESCADO (SEE RECIPE, P. 46)

Peel yuca and cut in 2-inch lengths. Cut the lengths in quarters vertically, and remove the thin, stringy core. Then cut yuca in small pieces and cover with water to prevent discoloration. Set aside. Purée corn and cilantro in a blender with one tablespoon water. Add more water (up to 3 tablespoons) as needed to make a purée. Set aside. Trim large pieces of fat from the meat and season with salt and pepper. Boil in 4 cups of water in a large, covered pot. When tender (about 2 hours), add the yuca and squash. Cook about 25 minutes over low heat until the yuca is soft and falling apart. The squash will have disintegrated. Add purée of corn and cilantro, stirring slowly over low heat for 15 minutes until sauce is thick. Correct the seasoning. Place each serving on a large plate, topped with some sauce. Garnish with scallion and red pepper and serve with rice topped with *ceviche de pescado*.

*Butternut squash is a substitute for the Peruvian squash *zapallo loche*.

Ají de Gallina

Shredded chicken in a flavorful cheese sauce with ground walnuts. Serves 6.
This classic dish, a national favorite, has many regional variations.

1 QUART WATER

1 TEASPOON SALT

1 4-POUND CHICKEN, QUARTERED

[Ají de Gallina, *continued*]

    1 CARROT, SLICED

    1 RED ONION, SLICED

    Pepper paste

    ½ CUP DICED RED ONION

    3 CLOVES GARLIC

    2 *AJÍES AMARILLOS,* DESEEDED AND DEVEINED*

    ½ CUP CHOPPED WALNUTS

    ¼ CUP WATER

    3 TABLESPOONS CORN OIL

    ¼ TEASPOON TURMERIC

    ¼ POUND PARMESAN CHEESE, SHREDDED (ABOUT 1 CUP)

    ½ LOAF SOFT WHITE BREAD (CRUSTS REMOVED), TORN
        INTO SMALL PIECES (ABOUT 2 CUPS)

    1 CUP EVAPORATED MILK

    1 TEASPOON SALT, OR TO TASTE

    ¼ TEASPOON PEPPER, OR TO TASTE

    6 TO 8 YELLOW POTATOES (YUKON GOLD, FOR EXAMPLE)

    3 HARD-BOILED EGGS, CUT IN QUARTERS

    6 BLACK OLIVES, CUT IN HALF LENGTHWISE

Bring salted water to a boil. Add chicken, carrots and sliced onion. Simmer for about 45 minutes, or until the meat is soft enough to shred easily. Remove the chicken and vegetables separately; strain the broth. Purée the vegetables and return to the strained broth. When the chicken is cool, shred the meat with two forks and set aside. In a food processor, blend diced red onion, garlic, *ajíes amarillos* and walnuts with water to form a smooth paste. Heat the oil in a small frying pan, and cook the pepper paste over low heat until golden. Add the turmeric, chicken, Parmesan cheese and 3 cups of the reserved broth, and bring to a boil. Soak the bread pieces in the evaporated milk for a few minutes until soft, then add the mixture to the chicken sauce. Stir over medium-low heat for about 10 minutes, or until the sauce is thick and creamy, but still pourable. Use the remaining broth to adjust the consistency if necessary. Add salt and pepper to taste. Boil potatoes with the skins on. When soft, peel the potatoes and slice in half lengthwise. Arrange on plates or a platter. Pour the chicken sauce over the potatoes. Garnish with eggs and olives.

*Despite the name (yellow chile pepper), this Peruvian chile pepper is orange. Frozen or bottled peppers may be substituted.

DESSERTS

Picarones

Doughnut-like fried dough made from pumpkin and sweet potato, drizzled in syrup.
Serves many.

This is the recipe for the *picarones* served at the Casa-Hacienda San José in Chincha. Celinda Reyes Farfán (see photo in color insert, second page, top right) has been making *picarones* for her happy customers for over 30 years.

5 OUNCES SWEET POTATO

½ POUND CANNED PUMPKIN

1 PACKET (¾ OUNCE) ACTIVE DRY YEAST

½ TEASPOON SUGAR

½ CUP WARM POTATO WATER

1⅓ CUPS FLOUR

⅛ TEASPOON SALT

VEGETABLE OIL FOR DEEP-FRYING

Syrup

½ CUP WATER

1 CUP DARK BROWN SUGAR

¼ CONE (2 OUNCES) *CHANCACA**

PEEL OF ½ ORANGE

2 STICKS CINNAMON

1 TEASPOON WHOLE CLOVES

1 TEASPOON ANISEEDS

Boil sweet potato until soft, reserving the cooking water. Peel and mash. Strain and mix with pumpkin in a bowl. To ½ cup of the potato water, cooled to about 100°F, add yeast and sugar and let sit 15 minutes. Add flour, salt and yeast mixture to the pumpkin and squash mixture. Beat well. Cover bowl with a damp towel and place in a 300°F oven for one minute. Turn off heat and leave bowl in oven for 45 minutes or until batter has roughly doubled in volume. While the dough is rising, combine syrup ingredients in a small saucepan and stir over low heat for 20–25 minutes. Strain and set aside. When batter has risen, heat vegetable oil to 325–350°F in a heavy pot. Have ready a finger bowl of water and ice cubes to help keep dough from sticking to your hands. Form balls about 2 inches in diameter. Poke a hole in the balls with your thumb and drop the rings into the hot oil. When golden on both sides, remove with a slotted spoon and drain. Serve *picarones* drizzled with syrup.

*Chancaca (also called *panela*) is hard, molded, unrefined sugar made by boiling sugar-cane juice until the liquid has evaporated.

Quinua Crepas con Aguaymanto Mermelada y Salsa de Naranja

Quinoa crêpes with cape gooseberry marmalade and orange sauce. Makes 5 crêpes.
This recipe was provided by Antonio Cossio Arana, chef/owner of Tunupa Restaurant in Cuzco and the Sacred Valley. (See photo in color insert, sixth page, bottom.)

¾ CUP QUINOA

1½ CUPS WATER

2 EGGS, WELL BEATEN

¾ CUP EVAPORATED MILK

6 TABLESPOONS FLOUR

1½ TEASPOONS VEGETABLE OIL

1 TEASPOON SALT

BUTTER

Filling

2 TABLESPOONS BUTTER

2 TABLESPOONS FLOUR

1 CUP MILK

1 CUP CAPE GOOSEBERRY (*AGUAYMANTO*) MARMALADE*

Orange sauce

1 TABLESPOON RED WINE

4 TABLESPOONS SUGAR

GRATED PEEL FROM 1 ORANGE

1 CUP ORANGE JUICE

1½ TEASPOONS RED WINE VINEGAR

Rinse quinoa in cold water until the water runs clear. Bring 1½ cups water to a boil and add quinoa. Cover and cook over medium heat for 12–15 minutes, until water level is below the level of the quinoa. Do not allow the water to boil off completely. Remove from heat and let sit 15 minutes. Mix crêpe ingredients together. For each crêpe, ladle a scant ½ cup onto a heated, lightly greased pan. Gently spread the batter to form a thin pancake. Cook over low heat until golden brown and firm enough to flip. Lightly brown the other side and set aside.

For the filling, make a roux with butter and flour over medium heat. Slowly add hot milk and cook over low heat, whisking continuously, until sauce thickens. Mix white sauce with ¾ cup marmalade. Top each crêpe with some filling and roll opposite sides up over it. Allow filling to gel while making orange sauce.

Caramelize sugar over low heat in a heavy pan and stir continuously until liquid and light brown. Add vinegar, orange juice and red wine, being careful of any spatters.

Bring to a boil and add orange peel. The sugar, which will have hardened and clumped, will go back into solution. Cook until sauce thickens. Add a little cornstarch dissolved in water to thicken, if needed. Before serving, top crêpes with some orange sauce mixed with ¼ cup marmalade.

Aguaymanto, cape gooseberry or ground cherry, a small, yellow-orange fruit encased in a papery husk. Substitute raspberry jam for a North American twist on this dish.

Arroz con Leche

Rice pudding. Serves many.

The recipe for this national favorite was adapted from *The Art of Peruvian Cuisine* by Tony Custer, who published his artful cookbook to fully fund the "Aprendamos Juntos" program that provides remedial support to children with learning disabilities in schools in the poorest sections of Lima (http://www.artperucuisine.com).

PEEL OF ½ LARGE ORANGE

1 CUP RICE

5 CUPS WATER

2 LARGE STICKS OF CINNAMON

2 CLOVES

1 CAN (14½ OUNCES) EVAPORATED MILK

2 CANS (28 OUNCES) SWEETENED CONDENSED MILK

¾ CUP RAISINS

1 EGG YOLK

½ CUP WHITE PORT

1 EGG WHITE

4 TABLESPOONS SUGAR

GROUND CINNAMON FOR DECORATION

PINCH SALT

Blanch orange peel in three changes of boiling water. Wash rice under running water until it runs clear. Put measured water in a saucepan with the orange peel, one cinnamon stick and cloves. Bring to a boil, then add rice, cover and simmer on low heat until all the liquid has been absorbed, about 30 minutes. Add evaporated milk and stir continuously. When the mixture returns to a boil, add condensed milk and raisins. Cook, stirring continuously, until the mixture thickens (about 10 minutes). Remove from heat and stir in egg yolk, ¼ cup Port and a pinch of salt. In a small, heavy pan, heat remaining Port and sugar to form a light syrup. Beat egg white until soft peaks form. Gently fold into the syrup and then into the pudding. Pour into individual serving dishes. Decorate with ground and stick cinnamon.

Miscellaneous

Pasta de Ají Amarillo

Yellow chile-pepper paste. Makes about 3 tablespoons.

3 AJÍES AMARILLOS, FRESH, FROZEN OR BOTTLED

Handle chile peppers carefully: their oils can irritate or burn the skin or eyes. Thaw frozen peppers. To remove skins, boil fresh or frozen peppers 1 minute and then transfer to ice water for about 1 minute. Peel with a paring knife. Bottled peppers peel easily without preparation. To make peppers less hot, remove seeds and veins. Cut fresh or frozen peppers in small pieces and boil in 1 cup water (½ teaspoon salt and 2 teaspoons vinegar, optional) for 5 minutes. Wash thoroughly in cold water. Repeat boiling and washing procedure. Drain. Bottled peppers do not require the boiling and washing steps. Grind peppers with 1 teaspoon water in a small blender to form a smooth paste. Freeze unused portion for later use.

Pasta de Ají Panca

Red chile-pepper paste. Makes about 2 tablespoons.

2 AJÍES PANCAS, DESEEDED AND DEVEINED

Fry peppers in a little oil for about 1 minute over medium heat, turning once or twice, being careful not to burn the pepper. Be sure to ventilate well while frying to remove pungent pepper fumes. Transfer pepper from frying pan to a small pan of boiling water. Remove from heat and use a heavy object to keep the pepper submerged for 1 hour. Then remove the pepper from the water, pat dry with paper towels and mash it to a paste with a mortar and pestle.

Salsa Criolla

Onion and chile-pepper salsa. Makes about 1 cup.

1 LARGE RED ONION

1 TEASPOON SALT

½ AJÍ AMARILLO, DESEEDED AND DEVEINED*

2 TEASPOONS VINEGAR

2 TEASPOONS VEGETABLE OIL

2 TEASPOONS KEY LIME JUICE

2 TEASPOONS CILANTRO, CHOPPED

Cut onion in half and thinly slice each half vertically in half-moon slices. Sprinkle with ½ teaspoon salt and let sit 5 minutes. Wash several times with cold water and drain. Sprinkle with remaining ½ teaspoon salt. Add *ají amarillo,* vinegar, oil, lime juice and cilantro, and mix well.

Shopping in Peru's Food Markets

Helpful Tips

Outdoor Markets

Travelers to Peru intent on experiencing the lively outdoor markets will learn a lot about Peruvian food, and at the same time gain valuable insight into Peruvian culture. Nothing brings strangers together more pleasantly than food, despite the existence of language barriers. Peru's villages and cities all told have a multitude of marketplaces with copious fresh produce and enthusiastic vendors to make such encounters almost certain.

Our favorite markets occur once a week in the countryside. Indeed, we juggle our itineraries so we can include as many weekly markets as possible. There is a tangible, heightened level of excitement between vendors as they enjoy gossiping with each other in the lulls between sales. Vendors heap their edibles in colorful, eye-catching piles to make purchasing them irresistible. Food generally is priced, but often not named. If you don't recognize an item, be prepared to ask, "What is this called?" (see *Helpful Phrases,* p. 77). If you intend to buy, don't haggle too much over the price. It is unlikely you will find cheaper prices or fresher food anywhere. Don't be surprised to see pens containing live guinea pigs, which soon will be selected for someone's frying pan. A typical preparation is *cuy chactado,* whole guinea pig flattened by a large stone during frying to provide even crisping. Since we consider guinea pigs pets, it's all a bit jolting. In coastal areas fishmongers hawk the catch of the day. The tangy smell of the sea is tossed in at no extra cost. A wide variety of non-food items will be found in another section of the market.

Smaller open markets operating daily include neighborhood stores and the many mobile and stationary carts of street vendors. There also are specialty stores selling only one type of food, such as fruits or vegetables. Smaller markets have higher prices and a reduced selection.

So many images in the markets beg for photographic capture. Some folks however, are reticent about having their picture taken. Always ask first.

The Indoor Markets

Food sold indoors is more expensive. Stores range from small neighborhood convenience shops to supermarkets—a more recent phenomenon—with a wide assortment of groceries and non-comestibles. You may be tempted to get the makings for a tasty picnic. Remember to pack some plastic tableware before leaving home!

The following abbreviated list of weights in Spanish proved sufficient to get the quantities we wanted. Corresponding approximate weights in ounces are included.

un décimo de kilo: 100 grams, or about a quarter pound (3.5 ounces)
un cuarto kilo: 250 grams, or about half a pound (9 ounces)
medio kilo: half kilo, or about one pound (17.5 ounces)

If you are considering bringing food back to the United States, obtain the Customs and Border Protection (CBP) brochure "Know Before You Go" to find out which agricultural items are allowed. The information is available online as a pdf file at http://www.cbp.gov/xp/cgov/travel/vacation/kbyg. You can also obtain a brochure by calling 1-877-CBP-5511. Listen to the menu and choose the option for ordering brochures. Be aware that websites do change, so you may have to go to the CBP homepage and click on "travel" to get to the webpage of interest if it has changed from the above.

A Health Precaution

Don't ask for trouble. Avoid eating food from street vendors. Some serious diseases can be transmitted by eating unclean produce. If you buy fruits and vegetables in the markets, make sure to wash them thoroughly with bottled water before eating. The safest fruits are those that can be peeled. Bottled water is readily available and is a wise choice, even in restaurants. Also, always brush your teeth with bottled water.

Resources

Online Suppliers of Peruvian Food Items

Many retail sources sell the special ingredients required for the recipes in this book. These ingredients are available in Latino food markets, other ethnic grocery stores such as Asian markets, natural and whole food stores, and large supermarkets. Good sources of fresh or (more likely) frozen banana leaves can be found in Asian and Latino markets.

Peruvian food items also can be purchased online from several websites. Since websites change their addresses or URLs and may not be updated regularly, you will probably need to do additional browsing. We suggest that you use your favorite search engine (our standby is google.com) and do a general search for Peruvian food markets or a specific search for a desired ingredient. We hope the following online businesses continue to offer fine Peruvian products for our readers.

El Mercado Grande sells several varieties of Peruvian chile peppers in sauce, paste or whole-pepper form. They also carry quinoa, sprouting corn (*maíz de jora*), canary beans (*fríjol canario* or *fríjol peruano*), dried potato bits (*papa seca*), white freeze-dried potatoes (*chuño blanco*), black freeze-dried potatoes (*chuño negro*), carob sauce (*algorrobina salsa*), dried purple corn on the cob (*maíz morado*), an herb called Peruvian black marigold (*huacatay*) and the cloying, bright yellow, bubble-gum flavored soda pop, *Inca Kola*.

El Mercado Grande
Mesa, Arizona
Tel: 480-862-2964
info@elmercadogrande.com
http://www.elmercadogrande.com

Amigofoods.com offers sauces and pastes of Peruvian peppers, corn beer (*chicha de jora*), canary beans (*fríjol canario*), dried potatoes (*papa seca*), large, dried, white lima beans or butter beans (*pallares*), as well as corn for toasting (*cancha*).

Amigofoods.com
7501 NE 3rd Place
Miami FL 33138
Tel: 800-627-2544
Fax: 516-627-0803
customerservice@amigofoods.com
http://www.amigofoods.com

Sanguineti Market has an online and storefront presence. Peruvian products available include flours of *chuño* (Andean freeze-dried potatoes), *camote* (sweet potato), *lúcuma* (fruit with firm, starchy flesh) and *faba* (fava) beans; Peruvian chile peppers in canned, dried, paste, and sauce form; beverages include *chicha morada* (non-alcoholic drink made with purple corn), soft drinks such as *Inca Kola,* nectars of *maracuyá* (passion fruit) and *maca* (sweet and spicy, radish-like tuber) and Peruvian coffee. Also available is *Sybarita,* a commercial mixture of powdered chile pepper, turmeric and other spices.

Sanguineti Market
7116 Blanco Rd.
San Antonio, TX 78216
Tel: 210-979-6439
Fax: 210-979-6704
email@sanguinetimarket.com
http://sanguinetimarket.com

Grow your own Peruvian chile peppers and cook with fresh chile peppers. The Chile Woman sells organically chile plants, including *ají amarillo, ají colorado, ají mono, ají panca* and *chinchi-uchu.*

The Chile Woman
1704 S. Weimer Road
Bloomington IN 47403
Tel: 812-339-8321
chilewmn@thechilewoman.com
http://www.thechilewoman.com

Some Useful Organizations to Know About

Peruvian Consulate in Chicago

180 N. Michigan Ave., Suite 1830
Chicago IL 60601
Tel: 312-782-1599
Tel: 312-853-6173/74
Fax: 312-704-6969
conperchig@aol.com
http://www.consuladoperu.com

International Organizations

We are supporters of two international organizations that promote good will and understanding between people of different cultures. These organizations, Servas and The Friendship Force, share similar ideals but operate somewhat differently.

Servas

Servas, from the Esperanto word meaning "serve," is a non-profit system of travelers and hosts. Servas members travel independently and make their own contacts with fellow members in other countries, choosing hosts with attributes of interest from membership rosters. It is a wonderful way to get to know people, be invited into their homes as a family member, share experiences and help promote world peace. For more information about membership in Servas, write or call:

US Servas Committee, Inc.
11 John St., Room 505
New York, NY 10038
Tel: 212-267-0252
Fax: 212-267-0292
info@usservas.org
http://www.usservas.org

The Friendship Force

The Friendship Force is a non-profit organization that also fosters good will through encounters between people of different backgrounds. Unlike Servas, Friendship Force members travel in groups to host countries. Both itinerary and travel arrangements are made by a member acting as exchange director. These trips combine stays with a host family and group travel within the host country. For more information on membership in The Friendship Force, write:

The Friendship Force
34 Peachtree St., Suite 900
Atlanta, GA 30303
Tel: 404-522-9490
Fax: 404-688-6148
info@friendshipforce.org
http://www.friendshipforce.org

Helpful Phrases

For Use in Restaurants and Food Markets

In the Restaurant

The following phrases in Spanish will assist you in ordering food, learning more about the dish you ordered, and determining what specialties of a region are available. Each phrase also is written phonetically to help with pronunciation. Syllables in capital letters are accented. Letters in parentheses are essentially soundless. You will discover that Peruvians heartily encourage your attempt to converse with them in Spanish. By all means, give it a try at every opportunity.

DO YOU HAVE A MENU?	¿Tiene el menú? *¿Tee-EH-neh ehl meh-NOO?*
MAY I SEE THE MENU, PLEASE?	¿Podría ver el menú, por favor? *¿Poh-DREE-ah vehr ehl meh-NOO, pohr fah-VOHR?*
WHAT DO YOU RECOMMEND?	¿Qué recomienda usted? *¿Keh reh-koh-mee-EHN-dah oos-TEHD?*
DO YOU HAVE . . . HERE? (ADD AN ITEM FROM THE MENU GUIDE OR THE FOODS & FLAVORS GUIDE.)	¿Tiene . . . ? *¿Tee-EH-neh . . . ?*

HELPFUL PHRASES

RESTAURANT

WHAT IS THE "SPECIAL" FOR TODAY?	¿Cuál es el "especial" de hoy?
	¿Kwahl ehs ehl "ehs-peh-see-AHL" deh (h)oy?
DO YOU HAVE ANY SPECIAL REGIONAL DISHES?	¿Preparan algún plato regional en especial?
	¿Preh-PAH-rahn ahl-GOON PLAH toh reh-he-oh-NAHL ehn ehs-peh-see-AHL?
IS THIS DISH SPICY?	¿Es picante este plato?
	¿Ehs pee-KAHN-teh EHS-teh PLAH-toh?
I / WE WOULD LIKE TO ORDER . . .	Me / nos gustaría ordenar . . .
	Meh / nohs goos-tah-REE-ah ohr-deh-NAHR . . .
WHAT ARE THE INGREDIENTS IN THIS DISH?	¿Cuáles son los ingredientes de este plato?
	¿KWAHL-es sohn lohs een-greh-dee-EHN-tehs deh EHS-teh PLAH-toh?
WHAT ARE THE SEASONINGS IN THIS DISH?	¿Cuáles son los condimentos de este plato?
	¿KWAHL-es sohn lohs kohn-dee-MEHN-tohs deh EHS-teh PLAH-toh?
THANK YOU VERY MUCH. THE FOOD IS DELICIOUS.	Muchas gracias. La comida es deliciosa.
	MOO-chahs GRAH-see-ahs. Lah koh-MEE-dah ehs deh-lee-see-OH-sah.

In the Market

The following phrases will help you make purchases and learn more about unfamiliar produce, spices and herbs.

WHAT ARE THE REGIONAL FRUITS AND VEGETABLES?

¿Cuáles son las frutas y los vegetales regionales?

¿KWAHL-es sohn lahs FROO-tahs ee lohs veh-hey-TAH-les reh-he-oh-NAH-lehs?

WHAT IS THIS CALLED?

¿Cómo se llama esto?

¿KOH-moh seh YAH-moh EHS-toh?

DO YOU HAVE . . . HERE? (ADD AN ITEM FROM THE FOODS & FLAVORS GUIDE.)

¿Tiene . . . ?

¿Tee-EH-neh . . . ?

MAY I TASTE THIS?

¿Podría probar esto?

¿Poh-DREE-ah proh-BAHR EHS-toh?

WHERE CAN I BUY FRESH . . . ?

¿Dónde puedo comprar . . . frescos?

¿DOHN-deh PWEH-doh kohm-PRAHR . . . FREHS-kohs?

HOW MUCH IS THIS PER KILOGRAM?

¿Cuánto cuesta un kilo de . . . ?

¿KWAHN-toh KWEH-stah oon KEE-loh deh . . . ?

I WOULD LIKE TO BUY ¼ KILOGRAM OF THIS / THAT.

Quiero comprar un cuarto de kilo de esto / esta.

Kee-EHR-oh kohm-PRAHR oon KWAHR-toh KEE-loh deh EHS-toh / EHS-tah.

MAY I PHOTOGRAPH THIS?

¿Podría tomar una fotografía de esto?

¿Poh-DREE-ah toh-MAHR OO-nah foh-toh-grah-FEE-a deh EHS-toh?

79

Other Useful Phrases

Sometimes it helps to see in writing a word or phrase that is said to you in Spanish, because certain letters have distinctly different sounds in Spanish than in English. You may be familiar with the word and its English translation but less familiar with its pronunciation. The following phrase comes in handy if you want to see the word or phrase you are hearing.

PLEASE WRITE IT ON MY PIECE OF PAPER.

Por favor escríbamelo en mi pedazo de papel.

Pohr fah-VOHR ehs-KREE-bah-meh-loh ehn mee peh-DAH-zoh deh pah-PEHL.

Interested in bringing home books about Peruvian food?

WHERE CAN I BUY A PERUVIAN COOKBOOK IN ENGLISH?

¿Dónde podría comprar un libro de cocina peruana en inglés?

¿DOHN-deh poh-DREE-ah kohm-PRAHR oon LEE-broh deh koh-SEE-nah peh-roo-AH-nah ehn een-GLEHS?

And, of course, the following phrases also are useful to know.

WHERE IS THE LADIES' / MEN'S RESTROOM?

¿Dónde están los servicios para damas / caballeros?

¿DOHN-deh ehs-TAHN lohs sehr-VEE-see-ohs PAH-rah DAH-mahs / cah-bah-YEHR-ohs?

MAY I HAVE THE CHECK, PLEASE?

¿Podría darme la cuenta, por favor?

¿Poh-DREE-ah DAHR-meh lah KWEHN-tah, pohr fah-VOHR?

DO YOU ACCEPT CREDIT CARDS? TRAVELERS CHECKS?

¿Aceptan tarjetas de crédito? ¿cheques de viajero?

¿AH-cehp-tahn tahr-HEH-tahs deh KREH-dee-toh? ¿CHEH-kehs deh vee-ah-HEH-roh?

Menu Guide

This alphabetical listing is an extensive compilation of menu entries in Spanish (and in some cases Quechua, the Inca language) with English translations to help make ordering food easier. In Spanish, **ch** is considered to be a separate letter, so entries beginning with **ch** appear separately after entries beginning with **c**. Likewise, **ll** and **ñ** alphabetize as separate letters after **l** and **n,** respectively.

Since you will encounter more than one spelling of many words on menus and elsewhere, we have cross referenced certain spelling variations for some words. For example, **v** and **b** may be used interchangeably in Spanish. Quechua words are transliterated in many different ways. The hard **k** sound may be spelled with a **c, k, q** or **qu.** If you have difficulty finding a word in this *Guide,* try spelling it phonetically to see the possible alternatives.

The *Menu Guide* includes typical Peruvian dishes as well as dishes that may only be available regionally. Because it was not feasible to list each entry in both Spanish and Quechua, the local name of a regional dish was used. Classic regional dishes that should not be missed are labeled "regional classic" in the margin next to the menu entry. Some noteworthy dishes popular throughout much of the country—also not to be missed—are labeled "national favorite." Of course, some regional classics are national favorites as well. Comments on some of our favorites also are included in the margin.

Peruvians begin their day with a light breakfast (*desayuno*) around 7 or 8 AM. *Almuerzo* is a larger meal taken in the late morning or early afternoon. In the country, supper (*cena*) is at 6 or 7 PM, but in Lima, restaurants typically serve dinner beginning at 8 or 9 PM. Not surprisingly, Peruvian restaurants range from small neighborhood eateries (*cafeterías, cevicherías, picanterías, quintas, pollerías* and *brasserías*) to upscale establishments in prestigious hotels in urban areas.

We hope you will use this *Menu Guide* in conjunction with the *Foods & Flavors Guide* to explore Peru's traditional *criollo* and *novoandino* cuisines with confidence. Try to sample as many of these fabulous dishes as you can on your next trip to Peru!

adobo de chancho pork marinated with a paste of the chile pepper *ají panca,* achiote, garlic, salt, and pepper. The liquid portion of the marinade may be wine, wine vinegar, corn beer (*chicha de jora*), or corn beer vinegar (*vinagre de chicha*). The marinade is diluted with enough water to cook the meat (with onions and other vegetables and herbs) and create a tasty reddish sauce that is soaked up with pieces of bread. Also called *chancho adobado* or *carne adobada.*

adobo de tortuga *adobo* or marinated meat dish made with turtle meat.

agrio vinaigrette flavored with unrefined sugar and chile peppers.

NATIONAL FAVORITE **aguadito** chunky main-course soup consisting of a grain (usually rice, but may be quinoa or pasta), vegetables (beans, corn, peas, yellow potatoes) and pieces of meat or seafood in a tasty stock.

REGIONAL CLASSIC **aguajina** beverage made from sweetened, puréed *aguaje* palm fruit.

aguaymanto sour variation on the *pisco sour* made with *pisco* (Peruvian brandy) that has been infused with *aguaymanto,* the Andean cape gooseberry or ground cherry, and includes some *aguaymanto* preserves. The cocktail is dusted with cinnamon.

ají de calabaza vegetarian stew of pumpkin or other winter squash, potatoes, fava beans, corn and cheese in a milk-based sauce flavored with chile pepper (*ají amarillo*).

NATIONAL FAVORITE **ají de gallina** shredded chicken in a thick, milk-based sauce made with chile pepper (*ají amarillo*) and ground walnuts. Typically it is served over yellow potatoes with garnishes of hard-boiled egg and black olives.

ají de lacayote *lacayote,* a sweet squash, and potatoes in a creamy sauce made with chile pepper (*ají amarillo*), fresh corn and fava beans.

ají de langostinos shrimp in a creamy yellow chile-pepper sauce, served over potatoes.

REGIONAL CLASSIC **ají de maní** spicy peanut sauce, served over yuca or *tacacho,* fried balls of mashed plantain. Also called *inchikuchu,* from the Quechua *inchik* (peanut) and *uchu* (chile pepper).

ají de mariscos mixed seafood in a creamy yellow chile-pepper sauce, served over potatoes.

ají de pescado fish in a creamy yellow chile-pepper sauce, served over potatoes.

ají picante condiment made from ground Brazil nuts, cilantro, flat-leaf parsley and chile peppers. Also called *uchucuta.*

NATIONAL FAVORITE **ajíaco** stew-like mixture of boiled potatoes flavored with onions, garlic, chile peppers, cheese and sometimes ground peanuts.

TOP LEFT *Lomo atún sobre pastel de choclo,* herb-coated tuna fillet atop a corn cake, served at Huaca Pucllana, Lima. **TOP RIGHT** *Causa de pulpa de cangrejo,* cold mashed potatoes layered with crab meat and avocado, served at Punta Sal, Lima. **MIDDLE** *Chita frita,* whole fish sliced in a cross-hatch pattern and deep fried, with *conchitas a la parmesana* on the side, served at El Tiradito, Lima. **BOTTOM** Gourmet chips from traditional varieties of Andean potatoes, a product developed to help sustain Andean cultures, International Potato Center (CIP), Lima.

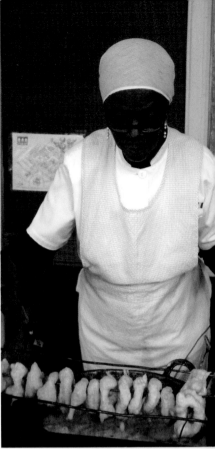

TOP LEFT *Cauche de camarones,* Peruvian-style fondue with river shrimp and yellow potatoes, made by chef Alcario Callyahua, Sol de Mayo, Arequipa. **TOP RIGHT** *Picarones,* doughnut-like fried dough made from pumpkin and sweet potato, prepared by Celinda Reyes Farfán, Hacienda San José, Chincha. **BOTTOM** *Pollo con salsa maracuyá,* chicken with passion fruit sauce, Inkafé, Sonesta Posadas del Inca, Yucay.

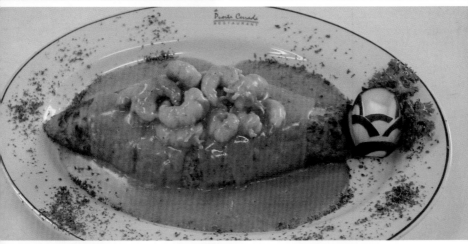

TOP LEFT *Cabrito a la norteña con fríjol redondo,* northern style kid with beans, served at La Perla de las Flores, Chiclayo. **TOP RIGHT** *Ponderación,* deep-fried, spiral-shaped pastry made on an iron mold, dipped in chocolate and topped with *lúcuma* ice cream, Map Café, Cuzco. **MIDDLE** *Tacu tacu en salsa de camarones,* fried patty of leftover beans and rice topped with shrimp, served at A Puerta Cerrada, Lima. **BOTTOM** *Ceviches de conchas,* scallops (in the shell) "cooked" with the Peruvian *limón,* a citrus fruit similar to the Key lime, served at La Bombonniere, Lima.

TOP LEFT *Camarones y pescado a la patarashca,* shrimp and fish in Patarashca style, served at La Patarashca, Tarapoto. **MIDDLE LEFT** *Tamalito verde,* savory corn tamale made green with spinach, served at El Rincón del Pato, Lambayeque. **MIDDLE RIGHT** Basket of fresh cheese for sale at a farmer's market, Lima. **BOTTOM** *Calamares rellenos,* stuffed squid, served at Wa Lok, a *chifa* (restaurant serving Chinese-Peruvian fusion cooking) in Lima.

TOP LEFT *Causa con pulpo al olivo,* cold mashed potatoes layered with octopus in olive cream, prepared by chef Maria de Lam, owner of Restaurant Huanchaco Beach, Huanchaco. **TOP RIGHT** Chorizo sausage proudly displayed by a vendor in Tarapoto. **BOTTOM** Market day in Pisac, one of the most colorful outdoor Indian marketplaces in the Andes.

TOP LEFT *Dulce de camote,* sweet potatoes in sugar syrup, served at El Catador restaurant and winery, Ica. **TOP RIGHT** *Carrillera de cerdo con puré de papa,* pork jowls with puréed potato, prepared by chef Rafael Piqueras, Sonesta Posadas del Inca, Lima. **MIDDLE LEFT** Pre-colonial *ceviche,* "cooked" with highly acidic *tumbo,* a passion fruit, served at Ñaylamp Restaurante, Lima. **BOTTOM** *Quinua crepas con aguaymanto mermelada,* quinoa crêpes with cape gooseberry marmalade, Tunupa Restaurant, Sacred Valley.

TOP LEFT Cucho la Rosa, director of the Cenfotur culinary program, displaying *ceviche de pescado,* fish "cooked" with the Peruvian *limón,* a citrus fruit similar to the Key lime. **TOP RIGHT** Sidewalk fruit cart tempting passersby in Lima. **BOTTOM** *Pescado sudado,* steamed fish, tomatoes, onions and chile pepper served with yuca at the Club Colonial restaurant, Huanchaco.

TOP *Lomo en salsa de sauco con tarta de quinua,* beef fillet with elderberry sauce and a quinoa tart, served at the Machu Picchu Pueblo Hotel, Machu Picchu Village. **MIDDLE** *Lomo saltado,* stir-fried dish of marinated beef strips with sweet and hot peppers, tossed with French fries, served at Manos Morenos, Lima. **BOTTOM LEFT** *King Kong,* a huge cookie filled with sweet milk caramel (*manjar blanco*) and fruit, a specialty of Chiclayo and Trujillo. **BOTTOM RIGHT** *Trucha apanada con papas huayro y humita,* breaded trout with native potatoes and a Peruvian tamale, served at Quinta el Eulalia, Cuzco.

The mixture can be served alone (see *ajíaco de papas*), but more often provides the foundation for chunks of chicken or some other meat.

ajíaco de cuy boiled guinea pig (*cuy*) seasoned with chile peppers, cumin, garlic, and vinegar and then fried to crisp the skin. The whole animal is served atop a spicy potato mixture (*ajíaco*).

ajíaco de ollucos (ullucos) sliced *olluco,* an Andean tuber, is substituted for potato in the classic *ajíaco.*

ajíaco de papas stew-like mixture of boiled potatoes, flavored with onions, garlic, chile peppers and cheese.

alfajorcito de Trujillo layered sandwich cookie from Trujillo that is a miniature version of the *King Kong,* with fillings of sweet milk caramel, pineapple and quince paste. See *King Kong, Foods & Flavors Guide.*

alfajores dainty pastry sandwiches made of two cookies with a filling of *manjar blanco,* a creamy, sweet milk caramel mixture. *Alfajores* come in a variety of sizes and typically are dusted with powdered sugar. In the jungle and other regions where yuca is prevalent, the cookies may be made with yuca flour, rather than wheat flour.   NATIONAL FAVORITE

algarrobina cocktail made with milk, egg white, carob syrup, and *pisco* (Peruvian grape brandy). It is served with ground nutmeg or cinnamon on top. See recipe, p. 44.   DELICIOUS

antecoco sweet made with coconut and milk, a Tumbes specialty.   REGIONAL CLASSIC

anticuchos appetizer or late-night street food of pieces of marinated beef heart, meat or fish grilled on skewers. The spicy marinade includes red wine vinegar, garlic, yellow or red chile peppers, cumin, salt, pepper and sugar. *Anticuchos* usually are served with beer or *chicha de jora* (corn beer) to counteract the heat of the spices.   NATIONAL FAVORITE

api de quinua hot breakfast drink made from ground quinoa cooked wih milk, cinnamon, cloves, vanilla and sugar.

arroz blanco white rice, typically molded and served on a separate plate.

arroz con leche creamy rice pudding with raisins and cinnamon, often with citrus and Port or sherry flavoring. See recipe, p. 69.   NATIONAL FAVORITE

arroz con mariscos rice with seafood.

arroz con pato rice with duck. Pieces of duck are cooked in dark beer (or *chicha de jora,* corn beer) with onions, garlic, chile peppers (*ajíes amarillos*) and other vegetables. The duck is served with rice colored green by large amounts of chopped cilantro and dotted with peas. The dish is typical of northern   REGIONAL CLASSIC coastal areas such as Chiclayo and Trujillo. Also called *arroz con pato a la chiclayana.*

arroz con pollo rice with chicken.

arroz chaufa Chinese-style fried rice.

arroz rojo red-colored rice. The color may come from achiote or red chile-pepper paste.

arroz tapado molded dish consisting of two layers of rice sandwiching a filling of beef sautéed with vegetables.

arroz verde con pollo green rice with chicken. Cilantro and spinach provide the green color in this flavorful side dish popular on the north coast.

arroz zambito caramelized dessert of rice with raw sugar (*chancaca*), nuts and raisins.

asado carne de res beef pot roast.

asado de cordero roast lamb. Also called *cordero asado.*

bacalao salt cod stew often prepared at Easter in Chincha.

batido de chocolate chocolate milk shake.

REFRESHING **batido de frutas** milk shake made with chopped fruit.

bien me sabe "tastes good to me," a dessert made with sponge cake, fruit, nuts and sugar syrup.

bisteck a la chorrillana beef fillets with *salsa chorrillana,* a sauce made with sautéed garlic, onion, chile pepper, red bell pepper, tomato, green peas and vinegar. Chorrillos is a coastal suburb of Lima.

bisteck de hígado de res beef liver steak.

bisteck de tortuga turtle steak.

bocados de quinua savory quinoa fritters.

bolitas de chocolate y coco sweet chocolate and coconut balls.

bolitas de oro balls of mashed sweet potato and yuca, flavored with cinnamon and anise, deep-fried and served with honey.

REGIONAL CLASSIC **bolitas de yuca** deep-fried balls of mashed yuca, which may include flour, egg and Parmesan cheese.

budín de chocolate chocolate pudding.

budín de maíz corn pudding.

buñuelos fritters.

TASTY **butifarra** sandwich made with spicy pork called *jamón del país.* A leg of pork, coated with garlic, onion, *ají amarillo* chile-pepper paste, and other spices, is simmered in stock until tender. Thin slices of the spicy, tender meat are piled on a sandwich roll and topped with *salsa criolla.*

cabrito a la norteña stew of kid meat in a thick sauce flavored with grated vegetables, cilantro, garlic, onions, and beer or corn beer (*chicha de jora*). It is served over rice with a side of beans. *Cabrito a la norteña* is a national favorite, but as kid is most readily available in the north, the dish is sometimes made with lamb elsewhere in Peru. This dish also is called *seco de cabrito* and *seco de cabrito a la chiclayana.* See recipe, p. 58, and photo in color insert, third page, top left. **REGIONAL CLASSIC**

cabrito al horno roast kid, a specialty of the northern city of Chiclayo. Also called *cabrito chiclayano.* **REGIONAL CLASSIC**

cacharrada mélange of fried organ meats.

cachito "little horn," crescent-shaped roll or cookie. The cookies are made with ground nuts and apricot jam.

café coffee.

café con leche coffee with milk.

caigua rellena stuffed pale-green, fleshy, hollow Peruvian squash. The squash may be stuffed with almost anything, including fish, chicken, beef or pork.

calamares a la milanesa breaded, fried squid.

calamares rellenos stuffed squid. See color insert for photo, fourth page, bottom.

caldo soup with a clear broth base.

caldo de bolas de banana meat-based broth with potatoes and banana balls. Green bananas or plantains are cooked, mashed, then formed into balls around a stuffing of finely chopped ground meat, onions, tomatoes, raisins, boiled eggs and olives. **REGIONAL CLASSIC**

caldo de carnero lamb and vegetable soup.

caldo de gallina estilo Cusco Cuzco-style hen soup, with yuca, rice, and potatoes. In Peru, hens generally are believed to have better flavor than roosters. **REGIONAL CLASSIC**

caldo de pollo chicken soup.

caldo de siete carnes soup with seven meats, which may include alpaca, beef, lamb, pork, chicken, llama, goat, turkey, or duck. **REGIONAL CLASSIC**

caldo verde green soup. Parsley and cilantro color this soup of potatoes and dried fish.

camarones a la plancha grilled shrimp.

camarones al ajo fried shrimp with garlic sauce.

REGIONAL CLASSIC   **camarones y pescado a la patarashca** shrimp and fish cooked in the Patarashca style—steamed with false cilantro (*sacha culantro*), onion and garlic in heliconium leaves.

camotes fritos French-fried sweet potatoes.

camotes rellenos mashed sweet potatoes stuffed with cheese and deep fried.

camotillo sweet-potato pudding spiced with cinnamon and nutmeg or almond extract. It is often served with colored candy sprinkles, nuts or raw sugar.

REGIONAL CLASSIC   **cancacho** suckling pig, lamb or guinea pig marinated in a chile-pepper sauce and roasted slowly for hours. *Cancacho* is a celebration food of Puno.

cangrejo reventado crab served atop a mixture of diced boiled potato, sautéed onion, garlic, chile peppers and seaweed, cooked with egg and wine or *chicha de jora* (corn beer).

canilla de cordero con puré de papas lamb shanks with puréed potatoes. See recipe, p. 52, and photo in color insert, sixth page, top right.

NATIONAL FAVORITE   **carapulcra (carapulca)** classic Andean pork and dried potato (*papa seca*) stew, flavored with ground peanuts, onion, garlic, cumin and plenty of chile peppers). Pork is a post-colonial substitute for guinea pig in this ancient dish. *Carapulcra* usually is served with a side of rice, yellow potatoes, or yuca, depending on the region. In Chincha, *carapulcra* often is served with *sopa seca,* a "dry soup" of pasta, vegetables and cheese.

carapulcra (carapulca) a la limeña Lima-style *carapulcra.* This variation on the classic dish includes both pork and chicken, has a bit of chocolate in the sauce, and is served with garnishes of hard-boiled egg, olives, farmer's cheese and parsley.

carne adobada see *adobo de chancho.*

carne arrollada beef tenderloin pounded flat, then rolled up with fillings of fried meats, boiled eggs, olives and onions. The stuffed meat roll is tied up, boiled until the meat is cooked, then served in slices like a jellyroll.

carne guisada stewed meat in a spicy tomato sauce.

carpaccio de pulpo octopus slices in an olive and mustard sauce, garnished with Parmesan cheese slices, green olives and capers.

caspiroleta eggnog-like cocktail made with *pisco* (Peruvian grape brandy), milk, egg, sugar, vanilla, nutmeg and cinnamon.

NATIONAL FAVORITE   **cau cau** tender pieces of beef tripe in a yellow sauce flavored with onion, garlic, chile pepper (*ají amarillo*), cumin, *palillo* (a turmeric-like food colorant), parsley and mint. The same dish is also called *cau cau limeña* (Lima-style *cau cau*) or, particularly in Chincha, *mondongo* (tripe).

cau cau de pescado *cau cau* with pieces of fish instead of tripe.

cauche de camarones thick, cheesy chowder with tomatoes, potatoes and river shrimp, flavored with onion, *huacatay* (a pungent herb) and parsley. See recipe, p. 50, and photo in color insert, second page, top left. REGIONAL CLASSIC

cauche de queso spicy cheese sauce served over boiled potatoes, typically offered in *picanterías,* small eateries that serve home-made *chicha de jora* (corn beer) and spicy snacks. REGIONAL CLASSIC

causa cold mashed potatoes layered with various fillings. There are many variations of *causa* from the color of the potatoes (typically yellow, but sometimes blue or green) to the spiciness of the flavorings (typically chile pepper, garlic, onions and Key lime juice), to the types of fillings (shrimp, crab meat, chicken salad, tuna salad, egg salad, avocado), to the shape of the *causa* (layered in a springform pan and served in wedges, rolled up like a jellyroll and sliced, layered in individual rounds, layered in a cake pan and cut in squares). Typical garnishes include olives, hard-boiled egg slices, pieces of seafood, chunks of cheese, sprigs of cilantro, or colorful mayonnaise sauces. *Causa* is served as an appetizer or for lunch. Also called *causa limeña*. NATIONAL FAVORITE

causa a la chiclayana a mound of flavored mashed potatoes served with fried fish, sweet potatoes, yuca, corn, plantains, boiled eggs, olives and cheese chunks. REGIONAL CLASSIC

causa colonial a *causa* variation in which the flavored mashed potatoes are rolled in balls and served with a hot-and-sour onion sauce and tempura-battered shrimp.

causa con pulpo al olivo cold dish of flavored yellow mashed potatoes layered with octopus in olive cream and topped with ground hard-boiled egg and chile peppers. See *causa*. Also see color insert for photo, fifth page, top left.

causa de pulpo de cangrejo cold dish of flavored yellow mashed potatoes layered with crabmeat. See *causa*. Also see recipe, p. 45, and photo in color insert, first page, top right.

causa de yuca con paiche cold dish of flavored mashed yuca layered with *paiche,* a large Amazon fish. This variation on the national favorite (see *causa*) uses ingredients more commonly available in the jungle. REGIONAL CLASSIC

causa limeña cold dish of flavored mashed potatoes layered with fillings. See *causa*.

cazuela soup with noodles and several kinds of meat and vegetables, typically peas, turnips, and carrots.

NATIONAL FAVORITE   **ceviche (cebiche)** chunks of raw, firm white fish (sole, flounder or tilapia, for example) "cooked" briefly in an acidic marinade, usually made with the Peruvian *limón,* similar to the Key lime. The dish also includes thin slices of red onion, usually washed in warm water and salt to reduce their pungency, slices of chile pepper (*ají limo* or *ají amarillo*) and salt. *Ceviche* typically is served on a bed of lettuce with chunks of boiled sweet potato and rounds of corn and is accompanied by *cancha* (toasted corn kernels). It is eaten any time of day, though more commonly in the morning and midday, and entire eateries, *cevicherías,* are devoted to creating only a wide variety of *ceviches.*

ceviche de conchas *ceviche* of scallops. See color insert for photo, third page, bottom.

REGIONAL CLASSIC   **ceviche de conchas negras** *ceviche* of black scallops, which grow in the coastal mangrove swamps in the department of Tumbes.

REGIONAL CLASSIC   **ceviche de pato cameño** Ancash-style *ceviche* of duck. Thin slices of duck meat are marinated in lime and orange juices prior to cooking with *pisco* (Peruvian grape brandy), onion, garlic, chile peppers, and other herbs and spices.

NATIONAL FAVORITE   **ceviche de pescado** fish *ceviche,* another name for traditional *ceviche* made with white fish. See recipe, p. 46, and photo in color insert, seventh page, top left.

ceviche en crema de rocoto *ceviche* served with a creamy sauce made from scallops, fish stock, puréed vegetables, and *rocoto* chile peppers.

ceviche mixto *ceviche* made with a mixture of seafoods, generally octopus, scallops, white fish, and shrimp.

coca sour *pisco* sour cocktail made with *pisco* (Peruvian grape brandy) infused with coca leaves. See *pisco sour.*

REGIONAL CLASSIC   **cocada** very sweet coconut dessert.

conchas al natural scallops served raw in the shell with a tangy sauce.

conchas asadas broiled scallops.

FABULOUS   **conchitas a la parmesana** scallops broiled in the shell with butter and Parmesan cheese.

conejo chactado seasoned rabbit flattened by a large stone during frying to provide even crisping.

cordero a la parrilla grilled lamb.

cordero asado roast lamb; also called *asado de cordero.*

costillar dorado "golden" fried ribs.

crema de ostiones oyster soup.

crema de papas cream of potato soup.

crema de zapallo cream of pumpkin (winter squash) soup. See p. 49 for a recipe for *crema de zapallo loche aromatizado de curry con conchas,* a curry-flavored cream of squash soup with scallops.

crema volteada flan or crème caramel. **NATIONAL FAVORITE**

cuchi canca suckling pig marinated overnight, then slowly roasted to develop a crispy skin and moist, tender meat. It is served with potatoes and salad.

cutacho balls of plantain mashed with ground peanuts, onion, garlic and false cilantro (*sacha culantro*). They often are served with hot coffee for breakfast or as an afternoon snack. **REGIONAL CLASSIC**

cuy al horno baked guinea pig. The village of Tipón near Cuzco has dozens of *cuyerías,* restaurants where guinea pigs are baked in large, domed outdoor clay ovens.

cuy asado roasted guinea pig.

cuy colorado guinea pig, cut in pieces and cooked in a red chile-pepper sauce with potatoes. The dish usually is garnished with olives and slices of boiled egg.

cuy chactado whole guinea pig flattened by a large stone during frying to provide even crisping. **CRUNCHY**

cuy frito fried guinea pig, which may be cooked whole or in pieces.

cuy relleno baked stuffed guinea pig. The stuffing is made from fried guinea pig viscera, onion, nuts, a variety of herbs and chile-pepper powder.

ch'airo Andean soup made with dried black potatoes (*chuño negro*) and as much meat (typically lamb intestines, dried mutton or alpaca) as a family can spare. The soup includes other starchy ingredients, such as peas, fava beans, barley, wheat berries, or corn, and root crops such as carrots or turnips. **REGIONAL CLASSIC**

chancho adobado see *adobo de chancho.*

chanfaina sautéed organ meats (kidney, liver, heart) with potatoes and rice.

chapana dessert made from sweetened grated yuca, sugar-cane brandy, raisins, annatto, and cloves, stuffed with banana slices and wrapped in steamed banana leaves. The ends of the leaves are twisted in opposite directions like a cellophane candy wrapper, and the packet is steamed. **REGIONAL CLASSIC**

chapo dish of ripe plantains mashed with fresh milk.

chicha de jora homemade corn beer. See *Foods & Flavors Guide.* **NATIONAL FAVORITE**

chicha de quinua fermented quinoa drink, similar to the *chicha de jora* made from corn.

REGIONAL CLASSIC   **chicha mochera**   Moche-style beer. This variation on *chicha de jora* takes its name from the Moche civilization that occupied what is now northern coastal Peru. It is made from a mixture of red and white corn and barley.

NATIONAL FAVORITE   **chicha morada**   refreshing nonalcoholic beverage made by boiling dried purple corn with pineapple skins and other fruits, cloves and cinnamon. See recipe, p. 44.

NATIONAL FAVORITE   **chicharrones**   small pieces of freshly deep-fried meat or fish, served hot (often with a dipping sauce) as an appetizer, snack or as part of a meal. Also called *fritadas*.

chicharrones de chancho   crispy deep-fried cubes of pork.

chicharrones y tocto de Saylla   crispy deep-fried cubes of pork with the skin still attached, made in the village of Saylla, near Cuzco. Quechua villagers wearing white stovepipe hats sell these hot *chicharrones* to tourists and other travelers along the road to Saylla.

REGIONAL CLASSIC   **chifles**   fried plantain slices; served as a sweet or savory snack.

chilcano   soup made with corvina or other white fish, garlic, Key lime juice, onion, parsley, and powdered red chile pepper (*ají panca*). *Chilcano* is named after the town of Chilca, near Lima, where it was created. It is considered a good hangover remedy.

chilcano de pisco   cocktail made with *pisco* (Peruvian grape brandy), ginger ale, Key lime juice and bitters. It is served in tall glasses with crushed ice and garnished with slices of lime.

chimichurri   condiment of Argentine origin, used as a marinade, basting sauce or dipping sauce. Traditionally made with corn oil, today it usually is made with olive oil. The specific ingredients vary, but always include garlic, salt and lots of parsley, with some combination of cilantro, oregano, *huacatay* (a pungent herb), onion, cumin, red pepper flakes, Key lime juice, red wine vinegar or balsamic vinegar.

REGIONAL CLASSIC   **chinguirito**   cocktail made with coconut water and *pisco,* Peruvian grape brandy. *Chinguirito* is also the name for a *ceviche* made from dried guitar fish, with fish broth included in the marinade.

REGIONAL CLASSIC   **chirimpico**   stew of chopped kid tripe with garlic, onions, chile peppers, grated winter squash (*loche*), cilantro and Key lime juice. Many preparations include corn beer (*chicha de jora*), liver or cooked blood. It is served with yuca and sweet potato.

REGIONAL CLASSIC   **chiriuchi**   cold plate with roasted guinea pig and many other kinds of meat, toasted corn, chunks of cheese, and omelets (*tortillas de huevos*). This meal is always served as part of the Catholic celebration of Corpus Christi in June (nine weeks after Easter) in Cuzco.

chita frita fish (*chita*) with firm white flesh sliced in a cross-hatch pattern on either side, then deep fried, with or without batter. It is served with various sauces and accompaniments. See color insert for photo, first page, middle.   **LOVELY**

choclo con queso corn on the cob (*choclo*) with a piece of farmer's cheese (*queso fresco*). It is also the name of a cooked dish made with grated corn, egg and cheese.

chocolate caliente hot chocolate.

chonta juane (chontafane) *juane* made of mashed hearts of palm. See *juane de chonta*.   **REGIONAL CLASSIC**

choritos seasoned Peruvian ribbed mussels (*choros*) with a sauce of onion, tomato, cilantro, corn, Key lime juice and salt.

choros a la criolla steamed Peruvian ribbed mussels, usually served on the half shell, topped with *salsa criolla*. Also called *choros a la chalaca,* or Callao-style mussels.

chulete de cerdo pork cutlet.

chunchulli juane (chunchullifane) *juane* made with mashed yuca, garlic, onions, cilantro and chile peppers stuffed with bits of hen meat and giblets. See *juane.*

chuño cola traditional Inca stew eaten on the coldest days. It is made with sausage, rice, chickpeas and potatoes and thickened with flour made from freeze-dried potatoes (*chuños*). A strip of dried llama "jerky" (*charqui*) often is served with *chuño cola.*   **REGIONAL CLASSIC**

chupe de camarones chowder with river shrimp, farmer's cheese (*queso fresco*), rounds of corn on the cob, potatoes, firm white fish, such as sole or flounder, chile peppers and eggs.   **NATIONAL FAVORITE**

chupe de cangrejo crab meat chowder.

chupe de mariscos de huanchaco seafood chowder from Huanchaco, near Trujillo in northern coastal Peru.

chupe de pallares verdes lima bean chowder made with corn rounds, spaghetti pieces, potato chunks, Asian dried shrimp, chunks of cheese, chile peppers, and eggs. See recipe, p. 51.   **REGIONAL CLASSIC**

chupe de papa seca chowder made in a base of milk, cheese, eggs, chile peppers and dried potatoes (*papa seca*).

chupe verde chowder made green with fresh herbs, including oregano, mint, *huacatay* (a pungent herb), cilantro and parsley. The chowder also contains potatoes, corn, cheese and eggs. Another name for this dish is *yacu chupe.*   **REGIONAL CLASSIC**

delicia de nueces nut delight. Dessert bars made with beaten egg whites folded into a dough of ground nuts, egg yolks, sugar and a small amount of flour. The bars may be topped with sweet milk caramel (*manjar blanco*).

DELICIOUS **dulce de camote** sweet potatoes in a fragrant sugar syrup with cinnamon, cloves and anise, decorated with colorful candy sprinkles. See color insert for photo, sixth page, top left.

dulce de coco sweet coconut balls.

dulce de zapallo sweet squash pudding.

empanadas de picadillo semicircular savory pastry filled with a mixture of finely chopped pork or chicken, olives, onion, boiled egg, raisins and chile peppers.

empanaditas de ajonjoli crescent-shaped cookies made with sesame seeds.

REGIONAL CLASSIC **ensalada de chonta** salad with long ribbons of shaved hearts of palm. Also called *ensalada de palmitos*.

REGIONAL CLASSIC **ensalada de palmitos** salad with long ribbons of shaved hearts of palm. Also called *ensalada de chonta*.

ensalada de pallares salad made with large white lima beans (butter beans).

ensalada de pallares verdes salad made with green lima beans.

ensalada de pulpo cold salad of chopped octopus, potatoes and olives.

REGIONAL CLASSIC **ensalada de sencca** cold salad of chopped beef nose, onion and *rocoto* chile peppers in vinaigrette.

ensalada de vegetales con vinagreta a variety of seasonal vegetables cooked and served on a platter with a bit of dressing.

ensalada mixta mixed vegetable salad.

ensalada rusa Russian salad. Potato salad made with cooked carrots and boiled eggs in a mayonnaise-based dressing. Peas, beets or apples are sometimes included.

NATIONAL FAVORITE **escabeche** "pickled" dish of sautéed fish or fowl marinated in vinegar with thin onion slices, chile peppers, garlic and other seasonings. The dish is served cold or at room temperature with garnishes of olives, boiled eggs and chunks of cheese.

REGIONAL CLASSIC **escribano** salad of potatoes, tomatoes, *rocoto* chile peppers and parsley in vinaigrette. This specialty of Arequipa is eaten plain or stuffed into traditional triangular rolls called *pan de tres puntas* (see *Foods & Flavors Guide*).

espesado de garbanzos thick purée of chickpeas.

espesado de lunes thick beef stew served on Mondays, particularly in Chiclayo. See *espesado de vacuno.*

espesado de res thick beef stew. See *espesado de vacuno.* Also called *espesado de lunes.*

espesado de vacuno beef chunks stewed in a sauce thickened with ground corn, grated winter squash (*loche*) and yuca. See recipe, p. 65. Also called *espesado de res* or *espesado de lunes.* NATIONAL FAVORITE

estofado de carne (de res) meat (beef) stew.

fríjol colado sweet paste of black or red beans cooked until thick with evaporated milk, brown sugar, and ground cinnamon, cloves and sesame seeds. REGIONAL CLASSIC

fríjol redondo canary beans seasoned with onion, garlic and chile-pepper paste, then partially puréed with milk. See recipe, p. 58.

fríjoles a la norteña northern-style canary beans. This creamy, yet piquant side dish is the traditional accompaniment of *seco de cabrito.* REGIONAL CLASSIC

fríjoles escabechados beans in a tangy sauce with vinegar, onions, chile peppers, bacon and beef ribs.

fritadas see *chicharrones.*

frito de chancho pork stir-fried with sweet potatoes and yuca, a typical breakfast food in the north.

frituras de plátano plantain fritters.

gallina al horno baked hen.

gallina enrollado Chinese-influenced dish of boneless chicken breast, flattened, seasoned with ginger and garlic, rolled up with a thin slice of ham, tied, dipped in egg, and flash fried in a wok. The fried rolls are simmered briefly in any of a variety of sauces before serving.

gallina tarmeña chicken stewed with potatoes, eggs, and rice, from the city of Tarma in the department of Junín. REGIONAL CLASSIC

gloriado cocktail made with sugar-cane brandy, cinnamon sticks, ground cloves and fig leaves. REGIONAL CLASSIC

guiso Spanish-influenced stew, typical of the north coast. REGIONAL CLASSIC

guiso de pato duck stew.

guiso de sangre de cordero stew with lamb and lamb's blood.

guiso de venado venison stew.

hígado de tortuga fried turtle liver.

hígados de pato saltado duck liver stir-fried with onions, tomatoes and French fries.

higos calados sugared figs.

REGIONAL CLASSIC **hornado** Andean-style roast pork. A whole pig is seasoned for several days before being slowly roasted in brick ovens. The roast has a crunchy, flavorful skin with moist, juicy meat.

REGIONAL CLASSIC **hualpa chupe** regional soup from Huancayo, a fragrant blend of chicken, chile peppers and achiote.

NATIONAL FAVORITE **huatia** pre-colonial, stewlike dish originally cooked in a hollowed squash or clay pot (*olla*) in a stone-lined pit in the ground. Today *huatia* is cooked in an *olla* over a fire (or in the oven).

huatia sulcana beef baked slowly in an oil, vinegar and red chile-pepper sauce with sliced onions, garlic, mint, oregano, rosemary, cilantro, *huacatay* (a pungent herb), cumin, oil and vinegar. It is served with baked sweet potatoes. See recipe, p. 61, and cover photo.

NATIONAL FAVORITE **humitas** Peruvian tamales. Chile-pepper flavored dough made with grated fresh corn is wrapped around a stuffing of a black olive, a piece of chicken, and a slice of hard-boiled egg. The dough is then wrapped in cornhusks and steamed. *Humitas* are eaten for breakfast and snacks and are sold in markets and by street vendors. See color insert for photo, last page, bottom right.

NATIONAL FAVORITE **humitas dulces** cornhusk packets filled with a sweetened corn mixture. Ground fresh corn is mixed with evaporated milk, lard or butter, sweetened with sugar or sweet milk caramel (*manjar blanco*) and stuffed with raisins or cheese. The cornhusk packets are then steamed.

humitas verdes green Peruvian tamales. See *tamalitos verdes.*

REGIONAL CLASSIC **inchikapi** chicken soup with ground peanuts, cornmeal, squash, yuca, onion, garlic and false cilantro (*sacha culantro*). The name comes from the Quechua *inchik* (peanut) and *api* (soup). Also called *inchikapi de gallina* and *sopa de gallina con maní.*

REGIONAL CLASSIC **inchikuchu** spicy peanut sauce, served over yuca or with *tacacho,* fried balls of mashed plantain. The name comes from the Quechua *inchik* (peanut) and *uchu* (chile pepper). Also called *ají de maní.*

inguiri boiled plantains.

jalea deep-fried seafood, potatoes and yuca, topped with *salsa criolla*. *Jalea* also is the word for jelly.

jamón serrano broad, thin slices of ham, steamed with onions and herbs. It is served on rolls with *salsa criolla*.

juane jungle food in which a filling (see specific entries for details) is placed on a pair of criss-crossed heliconium leaves (*hojas de bijau*). The flexible leaves are folded up and tied together with string or a palm fiber, then folded over and tied again. The whole packet is boiled, infusing the filling with the aroma of the jungle leaves. *Juanes* are eaten lukewarm or cold for breakfast and lunch in the jungle and are always part of the July 24th celebration of St. John the Baptist (*la fiesta de San Juan Bautista*), for whom they are named. The finished product, served on a platter, is meant to represent his head.   REGIONAL CLASSIC

juane de chonta *juane* made of mashed hearts of palm blended with onion, garlic, ground peanuts, ground corn, beaten egg, red bell pepper, false cilantro (*sacha culantro*) and other herbs. Pieces of *paiche* (a large Amazon fish) or a few shrimp are tucked into the center of the mixture. Also called *chonta juane*. See *juane*.   SO GOOD

juane de yuca *juane* made of grated yuca, seasoned with onion, garlic, false cilantro (*sacha culantro*), cilantro, and other herbs, mixed with small pieces of fresh or dried fish (typically *paiche*, a large Amazon fish) and some lard or oil. Also called *rumu juane*. See *juane*.

juane del arroz *juane* made of cooked rice colored yellow with turmeric or *palillo* (a turmeric-like food colorant), onions, garlic and other herbs, pieces of cooked chicken and black olives, mixed with beaten egg. Ground peanuts and yuca may be included the mixture, particularly in the jungle. See *juane*.

jugo de manzana apple juice.

jugo de naranja orange juice.

jugo de quinua thick, sweet drink made as a slurry of the Andean grain quinoa. It is typically served hot.

kapche soup with a base of fava beans, potatoes, eggs, milk and chunks of farmer's cheese (*queso fresco*), seasoned with onion, garlic, cumin and herbs such as oregano, *huacatay* (a pungent herb) and parsley.   REGIONAL CLASSIC

King Kong dessert consisting of a stack of huge cookies spread with sweet milk caramel (*manjar blanco*) and fruit fillings. See *Foods & Flavors Guide* and color insert, last page, bottom left.   REGIONAL CLASSIC

leche asada baked custard.

HITS THE SPOT   **leche de tigre** "tiger's milk," the marinade of a *ceviche. Leche de tigre* is served in a small glass as a hangover remedy. Kernels of toasted corn *(cancha)* are dunked in the juice using a tiny spoon. The salty crunch of the *cancha* in the tangy Key lime juice with the *ají* of the chile pepper is an indescribable combination.

lengua con puré tongue with mashed cheesy potatoes.

lenguado al vapor en salsa de maracuya steamed sole in passion-fruit sauce. See recipe, p. 54.

NATIONAL FAVORITE   **lenguado sudado** steamed sole. See *pescado sudado.*

REGIONAL CLASSIC   **locro** pre-colonial stew made with winter squash, potatoes, corn, onion, garlic, chile peppers, milk and cheese. Although often referred to as a stew, *locro* has the consistency of a casserole.

locro de zapallo creamy pumpkin stew.

lomo a lo pobre steak for the poor. A small portion of steak is stretched to serve six by including sausage, fried plantains, potatoes and eggs.

lomo atun en costar de hierbas peruanas sautéed tuna steak breaded with Peruvian herbs. See recipe, p. 56, and photo in color insert, first page, top left.

lomo en salsa de sauco beef tenderloin in elderberry sauce. See recipe, p. 63, and photo in color insert, last page, top.

NATIONAL FAVORITE   **lomo saltado** marinated strips of beef stir-fried with red onion, tomatoes, red bell peppers and chile peppers *(ajíes amarillos),* then tossed with hot French fries and served with rice. See color insert for photo, last page, middle.

llunca de gallina chicken soup with wheat berries.

machacado de membrillo cinnamon-flavored quince paste formed into bars and sold as a sweet treat.

majado de yuca con chicharrón mashed yuca with fried pork.

majarisco plantains cooked in a sauce of mixed shellfish.

REGIONAL CLASSIC   **mala rabia** "evil rage." The components of this dish—rice, peas, mashed ripe bananas mixed with crumbled fresh goat cheese, and cubes of dried fish in a mixture of corn beer *(chicha de jora)* and vinegar—are arranged separately on a single platter.

mantecado cookies made with lard, egg yolks and sugar. The name comes from *manteca de cerdo,* pork lard.

mariscos saltado mixed seafood stir-fried with red onion, tomatoes, red bell peppers and chile peppers (*ajíes amarillos*), then tossed with hot French fries and served with rice. Also called *saltado de mariscos.*

masato beverage made in the jungle from fermented yuca with sweet potato or sugar. Drinks made by fermenting *pijuayo,* the fruit of the peach palm, or other starchy foods may also be referred to as *masato.*   REGIONAL CLASSIC

mate de coca coca tea, recommended in the Andes to prevent altitude sickness.   REGIONAL CLASSIC

mazamorra de leche thick milk pudding; blancmange.

mazamorra de quinua thick milk-based pudding similar to tapioca or rice pudding, but with quinoa as the starchy grain.

mazamorra morada deep purple-black dessert made from purple corn, sugar and dried fruits. It is thickened with sweet-potato flour and spiced with cinnamon, cloves and aniseed.   NATIONAL FAVORITE

milanesa de pescado Italian-style fish fillets. The fish is coated in flour, egg and bread crumbs, then fried. Also called *pescado a la milanesa.*

milanesa de pollo Italian-style breast of chicken. The meat is flattened, coated in flour, egg and bread crumbs, then fried. Also called *pollo a la milanesa.*

mondongo hearty tripe stew. See *cau cau.*   NATIONAL FAVORITE

moqueguano de camarón shrimp in the shell with seaweed.

morusa purée of white lima beans mixed with beef or pork, garlic and onions.   REGIONAL CLASSIC

natillas cold custard. Also called *natillas de leche.*   REGIONAL CLASSIC

nina juane grilled *juane* made with pieces of boiled young chicken, partridge, or other fowl blended with beaten egg, onion, garlic, false cilantro (*sacha culantro*) and other herbs. See *juane.*

no es nada "nothing at all." It is a dessert pudding made from evaporated milk, egg yolks, sugar and vanilla.

ocopa small boiled potatoes covered with *salsa de ocopa*, a sauce made with ground, roasted peanuts, evaporated milk, cheese, soda crackers (or bread), onions, garlic, chile peppers and *huacatay* (a pungent herb). Some preparations include puréed shrimp in the sauce. Also called *ocopa arequipeña.*   REGIONAL CLASSIC

NATIONAL FAVORITE   **olluquito** finely julienned bits of the starchy Andean tuber *olluco* sautéed with onions, garlic and chile peppers, then cooked with any of a variety of meats. Parsley is added in the final stages of cooking. This national dish of Peru is served with rice.

olluquito con charqui *olluquito* with shredded dried meat (jerky); see *olluquito.*

orines del niño "little boy's pee" is a less-than-appetizing name for this refreshing drink made from pineapple juice, white grape juice, *pisco* (Peruvian grape brandy), cinnamon, cloves, and finely chopped apple and mango.

NATIONAL FAVORITE   **pachamanca** from the Quechua words for earth and cooking pot, *pachamanca* is a mixture of meats, potatoes and vegetables cooked with extremely hot volcanic stones in a covered pit in the ground. Originally an Andean tradition celebrating the harvest in February and March, this feast dish now is available throughout the year and throughout Peru.

REGIONAL CLASSIC   **paiche a la loretana** fillet of *paiche,* a large Amazon fish, served with fried yuca and plantains and a salad of shredded palm hearts.

palitos de yuca deep-fried sticks of cooked yuca—a yuca French fry. Typically served with *salsa huancaina.*

pango de pescado con plátano dish of fish and plantains with no seasoning other than salt.

NATIONAL FAVORITE   **papas a la huancaina** boiled yellow potatoes, sliced in half, served on a bed of lettuce, covered with a cold yellow sauce of cheese, evaporated milk, oil, Key lime juice, chile pepper, crushed crackers, onion, garlic, salt and pepper, blended until creamy. The dish is garnished with black olives, quartered hard-boiled eggs and rounds of corn on the cob. This appetizer and luncheon dish originated in the Andean city of Huancayo. See recipe, p. 47.

papas a la huancaina estila chiclayano Chiclayo-style *papas a la huancaina.* In this variation on the classic dish, the potatoes are mashed and formed into balls, not sliced. See *papas a la huancaina.*

papas con charqui boiled potatoes with beef or alpaca "jerky."

NATIONAL FAVORITE   **papas rellenas** mashed yellow potatoes mixed with egg, re-formed into a potato shape around a filling of seasoned ground meat, and deep fried. The dish typically is served with *salsa criolla.*

NATIONAL FAVORITE   **parihuela** fisherman's soup. Mixed seafood in a fish broth flavored with chile peppers, tomatoes, onions and *chicha*, beer, wine or *pisco* (Peruvian grape brandy). The soup develops a gelatinous consistency as the fish cartilage cooks.

parrilladas mixed grilled meats.

pastel de choclo moist, savory cake made with fresh corn and eggs. Some versions have a lower layer of ground meat, raisins, chile peppers, onion and other seasonings. See recipe, p. 56.

pastel de papas baked dish of sliced potatoes with cheese and evaporated milk. The crunchy top contrasts nicely with the creamy layers below. *Pastel de papas* is a specialty of Arequipa. **REGIONAL CLASSIC**

pastel de tres leches "three milk cake." See *torta de tres leches.*

pastelillos de yuca yuca sweets. A ball of dough made with yuca and aniseed is filled with sweet milk caramel or sweet potato cream. The dough is sealed around the filling and flattened into a rough star shape before being deep fried. The golden pastries are served hot sprinkled with powdered sugar and cinnamon.

patacones twice-fried plantains. Slices of plantains are fried lightly, then drained, flattened, and fried again to brown and crisp. Served while hot and soft. Also called *tostones.* **REGIONAL CLASSIC**

patarashca fish (typically *paiche* or *dorado*), roasted in a packet of heliconium leaves with chopped tomato, red bell pepper, garlic, onion, false cilantro (*sacha culantro*) and other herbs. The vegetable juices steam the fish. Also called *pescado de patarashca.* See color insert for photo, fourth page, top. **REGIONAL CLASSIC**

patasca soup of tripe, cow's feet, corn, onion, garlic, herbs and spices. Preparations vary and may include additional meats, potatoes, tomato, chile peppers, wheat berries, quinoa or beans. **REGIONAL CLASSIC**

patitas con maní pig's feet (*patitas de cerdo* or *patitas de chancho*) or cow's feet (*patitas de vaca*) and potatoes in a spicy peanut sauce.

patitas de chancho en fiambre cold dish of pig's feet in a vinegary onion and chile-pepper sauce. This *escabeche* is served with yuca. Also called *patitas en fiambre.*

patitas en fiambre see *patitas de chancho enfiambre.*

pato asado roast duck.

pato saltado a la paisana peasant-style stir-fried duck and vegetables, which often is served after a first course of *humitas.*

pecan caldo lamb's head soup with tripe, spiced with mint, parsley, cilantro and garlic. **REGIONAL CLASSIC**

pepián de cuy fried pieces of guinea pig cooked in a sauce with onions, chile peppers and ground, roasted peanuts. It is served with potatoes and rice.

pepián de choclo ground fresh corn cooked with sautéed onion, garlic, chile peppers and other seasonings to form a soft "pudding." Some preparations include cheese. In the north, small pieces of pork are often incorporated.

pepián de pavo turkey, marinated and roasted, and ground fresh corn cooked with sautéed chile pepper, onion, garlic, cilantro and other herbs to form a soft "pudding." In the north, ground rice may substitute for corn.

pernil a la criolla creole-style fresh pork shoulder. The skin is removed and the meat is marinated overnight with a dry rub (*aliño*) applied through dozens of cuts down to the bone. The rub includes cloves, allspice and cinnamon. The meat is cooked slowly and basted with the juices.

SUCCULENT **pernil al horno** fresh pork shoulder that has been marinated overnight with a dry rub (*aliño*) applied through dozens of cuts down to the bone. The rub includes garlic, oregano and pepper with just enough oil and vinegar to hold it together. The meat is cooked slowly and basted with the juices.

pescado a la chorrillana fillets of steamed white fish covered in *salsa chorrillana,* a sauce made with sautéed garlic, onion, chile pepper, red bell pepper, tomato, green peas and vinegar. Chorrillos is a coastal suburb of Lima.

pescado a la milanesa Italian-style fish fillets. See *milanesa de pescado.*

pescado a lo macho sautéed fillet of white fish served *a lo macho,* in a creamy, piquant sauce of tomatoes, chile peppers and chopped shellfish. The dish typically is served with rice.

REGIONAL CLASSIC **pescado de patarashca** fish (often *paiche* or *dorado*), roasted in a packet of banana or heliconium leaves with chopped tomato, red bell pepper, garlic, onion, false cilantro (*sacha culantro*) and other herbs. The vegetable juices steam the fish. Also called *patarashca.*

NATIONAL FAVORITE **pescado sudado** fillets of tilapia, sole, corvina or other firm white fish steamed over onions and tomatoes, with chile pepper, cilantro and Key lime juice. Also called *sudado de pescado.* See recipe, p. 55, and photo in color insert, seventh page, bottom.

pesque de quinua purée of quinoa cooked with milk and small cubes of farmer's cheese (*queso fresco*).

picante de camarones shrimp in a chile-pepper sauce.

picante de cuy guinea pig served in a chile-pepper sauce.

picante de choclo ground fresh corn in a chile-pepper sauce.

picante de mariscos mixed seafood in a chile-pepper sauce.

picante de pescado chunks of *cojinova,* pompano or other semi-fat fish, marinated briefly in lemon juice, garlic paste and chile-pepper paste, then cooked with boiled potatoes or yuca in a sauce made from sautéed onion, tomatoes and peanut purée.

picarones doughnut-like snack or dessert made from a yeasty pumpkin dough. The rings of dough are formed by hand, deep-fried and served with a raw-sugar syrup flavored with orange, aniseed, cinnamon and cloves. See recipe, p. 67, and photo in color insert, second page, top right. **REGIONAL CLASSIC**

pie de chocolate chocolate pie.

pie de limón Key lime pie.

pie de manzanas apple pie.

pisco sour national cocktail of Peru made with *pisco* (Peruvian grape brandy), Key lime juice, sugar syrup, egg white and ice. See recipe, p. 43. Variations can be made with *pisco* that has been steeped with macerated fruits or herbs. **NATIONAL FAVORITE**

plato huanchaquero appetizer made with potatoes and seaweed harvested off Huanchaco beach near Trujillo.

pobre de tres carnes stew of three meats with yuca, potatoes, rice and chopped vegetables. The dish often is served during *semana santa,* the holy week leading up to Easter.

pollo a la brasa spit-roasted chicken, available at *pollerías* and *brasserías,* restaurants specializing in rotisserie chicken. **NATIONAL FAVORITE**

pollo a la milanesa Italian-style breast of chicken. See *milanesa de pollo.*

pollo con salsa maracuyá chicken with passion-fruit sauce. See color insert for photo, second page, bottom.

pollo dorado "golden" fried chicken.

ponderación delicate deep-fried pastry spiral made on an iron mold. See color insert for photo, third page, top right. **ELEGANT**

poroto sherumbi soup made with fresh or dried beans, corn, chopped yuca, garlic, onion and *sacha culantro* (false cilantro). Also called *sopa nativa.*

puchero a one-dish stew with beef, pork, lamb, potatoes, cabbage, garlic, onions and other root vegetables, such as carrots and *arracacha.* **REGIONAL CLASSIC**

puchkuy leavened "bread" made from yuca, cornmeal, sugar (refined and raw) and eggs, baked in banana leaves and served for breakfast or afternoon tea in the jungle. **REGIONAL CLASSIC**

pulpo al oliva sliced octopus with olive sauce.

puré de pallares fresh or dried, rehydrated white lima beans (also called butter beans), cooked until soft, then puréed with butter, Parmesan cheese and cream.

puré de papas boiled potatoes puréed with butter, Parmesan cheese and cream.

puspu boiled fresh fava beans, served as a snack or appetizer.

queso helado "cheese ice cream," an iced milk dessert that is not really made from cheese.

quinotto "risotto" using quinoa in place of rice. See recipe, p. 62.

quinua atamalada dish of quinoa, tomatoes, cheese and sometimes potatoes.

quinua crepas con aguaymanto mermelada dessert of quinoa crêpes topped with a cape gooseberry filling. See recipe, p. 68, and photo in color insert, sixth page, bottom.

quinua en salpicon cold salad, similar to tabouli, but with quinoa substituting for bulgur wheat. Includes chopped tomatoes, cucumber, parsley, and mint in a citrus vinaigrette.

ranfañote cooked dessert made from raw sugar or molasses, walnuts, farmer's cheese, cloves, aniseed and cubes of French bread. It is served cold.

REGIONAL CLASSIC **raya guisada** stew made with chunks of ray or skate with onions, garlic, chile pepper, cilantro, Key lime and sour orange juice.

refresco de uvas fresh-squeezed grape juice with Key lime and orange juice, finely chopped pineapple and a dash of nutmeg.

relleno iqueño Ica-style blood sausage.

NATIONAL FAVORITE **rocoto relleno** hot *rocoto* pepper stuffed with a tasty ground-meat filling, topped with a melting cheese, and baked. Some preparations include a quarter of a boiled egg and a slice of boiled potato with the meat filling. It is found throughout Peru, but is a specialty of Arequipa and Cuzco.

REGIONAL CLASSIC **rompope** eggnog-type cocktail made with milk, sugar, egg yolks, *pisco* (Peruvian grape brandy), vanilla, cinnamon and cloves.

rosquita de manteca crunchy, ring-shaped pastry. The dough is made from flour, sugar, lard, salt and aniseed. In the jungle, they usually are made with yuca flour and are called *rosquetes*.

rumu juane *juane* made with grated yuca and fish. See *juane de yuca*.

rumu kusashqa grilled yuca, which is called *yuca a la brasa* in Spanish.

rumuapi dried or fresh *paiche* (a large Amazon fish) in a green   REGIONAL CLASSIC
soup made from puréed yuca, chile peppers, onion, garlic,
cilantro and false cilantro (*sacha culantro*), which supply the
color. Some preparations include puréed plantain. The name
comes from the Quechua *rumu* (yuca) and *api* (soup). The
Spanish name for this dish is *sopa de yuca con paiche*.

salpicon salad of shredded lettuce and diced beef (or other meat)   REGIONAL CLASSIC
with other raw vegetables, typically carrots, onions, tomatoes
and parsley in vinaigrette.

salsa criolla simple onion salad served as a condiment with many   NATIONAL FAVORITE
dishes. It includes thin slices of red onions (rinsed to reduce
their pungency), chile pepper, Key lime juice, vinegar, olive oil
and salt. Also called *salsa de cebolla, sarza* and *zarsa*. See recipe,
p. 70.

salsa chorrillana sauce from the Lima suburb of Chorrillos that is
made with sautéed garlic, onion, chile pepper, red bell pepper,
tomato, green peas, vinegar, and a little flour.

salsa de huacatay sauce made with *huacatay* (a pungent herb in
the marigold family), chile peppers, oil and vinegar. The sauce
is served as an accompaniment with meat, fish and potatoes.

salsa de maní peanut sauce.

salsa de ocopa classic sauce of Arequipa, made with ground,   REGIONAL CLASSIC
roasted peanuts, evaporated milk, cheese, soda crackers or
bread, onions, garlic, chile peppers and *huacatay* (a pungent
herb). The sauce typically is served at room temperature over
boiled potatoes as a first course, but may be served over yuca or
river shrimp (*camarones*).

salsa de rocoto sauce made with *rocoto* chile peppers.

salsa huancaina cold yellow sauce of cheese, evaporated milk, oil,
Key lime juice, chile pepper, onion, garlic, salt and pepper,
blended until creamy.

saltado de mariscos stir-fried seafood. See *mariscos saltado*.

saltena de pollo chicken and vegetable pie.

saltero de queso zarza farmer's cheese salad, which includes
cheese cubes, onion, hard-boiled egg, tomato, parsley, white
wine vinegar and Key lime juice.

sancochado meat and vegetable soup. *Sancochado* typically has   NATIONAL FAVORITE
boiled beef (although pork, fish and chicken may also be used)
and lots of vegetables, including carrots, turnip, celery, onion,
garlic, yuca, potatoes, rounds of corn on the cob, cabbage and

sweet potatoes. In the north, *sancochado* is less likely to include sweet potatoes. Preparations in the jungle may include plantains. The boiled meat and vegetables are served on a platter separately from the broth.

sango sweet pudding made with corn flour, lard and raisins, flavored with cloves and aniseed.

sango de trigo sweet pudding made with whole-wheat flour, raisins and walnuts.

REGIONAL CLASSIC **sangrecita** chicken blood cooked with onion, chile peppers, parsley and cilantro, served with kernels of cooked corn.

sangrecita de cabrito a la trujillana Trujillo-style *sangrecita* (made with suckling goat). Dish of roast kid meat, offal and blood, cooked with diced potatoes, onion, chile peppers, mint and cilantro. It is served with yuca and *salsa criolla*.

sanwich de pavo turkey sandwich.

sar de patita cold salad of chopped pig's feet, onions, potatoes and parsley. Also called *zarza de patitas de chancho*.

REGIONAL CLASSIC **sarapatera** Amazon turtle soup served from the shell. The meat of a large (60 to 100 pounds) turtle is cooked with mashed plantains, yuca, garlic and false cilantro (*sacha culantro*) in the turtle shell.

NATIONAL FAVORITE **sarsa** see *salsa criolla*. Also spelled *zarza*.

REGIONAL CLASSIC **seco de cabrito** "dry" stew of kid meat. The sauce is thickened with grated vegetables, and flavored with cilantro, garlic, onions, and corn beer. It is served over rice with a side of beans. *Seco de cabrito* is a national favorite, but as kid is most readily available in the north, the dish is sometimes made with lamb elsewhere in Peru. The dish also is called *seco de cabrito a la chiclayana* and *cabrito a la norteña*. See recipe, p. 58.

seco de carne meat (usually beef) cooked in a "dry" sauce that is thickened with a variety of grated vegetables.

REGIONAL CLASSIC **seco de chavelo** green bananas grilled with dried, salted meat (*cecina*), then tossed with a mixture of garlic, onion, tomato, chile pepper (*ají panca*), cumin, salt and vinegar.

seco de res beef chunks cooked in a "dry" sauce thickened with a variety of grated vegetables.

NATIONAL FAVORITE **shambar (chambar)** soup made with wheat berries, lentils, peas, chickpeas, chile peppers (*ajíes amarillos*) ham, and ham bones. The heat of the chile peppers in the soup is nicely balanced by the refreshing mint and cilantro.

REGIONAL CLASSIC **solterito arequipeño** salad from Arequipa made with fava or broad beans, fresh corn kernels, olives, farmer's cheese (*queso fresco*) and Key lime juice. Also called *soltero*.

sopa a la criolla vegetable soup with beaten egg, evaporated milk, noodles and small chunks of beef.

sopa de fríjol yellow bean and two-meat stew.

sopa de gallina con maní chicken soup with ground peanuts, cornmeal, squash, yuca, onion, garlic and false cilantro (*sacha culantro*). Also called *inchikapi* and *inchikapi de gallina*.   REGIONAL CLASSIC

sopa de maíz corn soup, made with milk, cheese and chile peppers.

sopa de novia "bride's soup." Broth with sautéed onion, garlic and slivers of black olive, served with croutons and chile peppers.

sopa de trigo beef chunks and whole-wheat kernels in broth with vegetables and herbs.

sopa de yuca con paiche dried or fresh *paiche* (a large Amazon   REGIONAL CLASSIC fish) in a green soup made from puréed yuca, chile peppers, onion, garlic, cilantro and false cilantro (*sacha culantro*), which supply the color. Some preparations include puréed plantain. The Quechua name for this dish is *rumuapi,* yuca soup.

sopa nativa soup made with fresh or dried beans, corn, yuca, garlic, onion and false cilantro (*sacha culantro*). Also called *poroto sherumbi.*

sopa seca "dry soup." *Sopa seca* begins with pasta sauteed in oil.   REGIONAL CLASSIC It is then cooked in a sauce of chicken broth, tomatoes, onions, garlic, chile peppers and cilantro until the pasta is tender and the liquid is absorbed. It is served with grated cheese on top. In Chincha, *sopa seca* is often served with *carapulcra,* a diced pork and dried potato stew.

sopa teóloga (sopa teológica) soup made with turkey or chicken   REGIONAL CLASSIC hen, lentils, tomatoes, onions, chunks of bread, chile peppers and other seasonings, including saffron, turmeric or *palillo* (a turmeric-like food colorant) to make it yellow. It is served with rice and garnished with hard-boiled eggs and sliced olives.

sudado de pescado steamed white fish. See *pescado sudado.*   NATIONAL FAVORITE

suspiro meringue cookie "sigh."

suspiro a la limeña "Lima sigh." Sweet milk caramel pudding   REGIONAL CLASSIC with a Port-flavored meringue topping. Also called *suspiro de limeña.*

tacacho fried or grilled balls of mashed plantain. *Tacacho* is often   REGIONAL CLASSIC served with *cecina* (seasoned, dried meat) and *inchikuchu,* a sauce of ground, roasted peanuts and chile peppers.

tacu tacu mixture of leftover beans and rice, flavored with onion,   NATIONAL FAVORITE garlic, chile-pepper paste and pork fat, and fried into a patty or tapered tube. It can be dressed up with a seafood filling and sauce, served alongside steak or liver, or topped with a fried egg (*tacu tacu montado*).

tacu tacu de pallares en salsa de camarones *tacu tacu* made with white Lima beans (butter beans) and served with river shrimp (*camarones*) in a white-wine sauce. See recipe, p. 60, and color insert, third page, middle.

tallarines con culantro spaghetti in a green cilantro-flavored sauce.

tallarines verde spaghetti in a green pesto-like sauce made with spinach, basil, ground walnuts and cheese. Also called *tallarines en salsa verde*.

NATIONAL FAVORITE **tamal criollo** tamale with a dough of ground dried corn (*maíz mote*) mixed with oil, chile-pepper paste, garlic and cumin seeds. The dough is placed on a banana leaf and topped with one slice each of cooked pork, chile pepper and hard-boiled egg, olives and roasted peanuts. The banana leaf is folded over the mixture to form a rectangular parcel, which is tied with twine and simmered in water.

REGIONAL CLASSIC **tamal chinchano** Chincha-style red tamale. Chile-pepper paste and achiote color the pork-stuffed corn dough that is wrapped in cornhusks and steamed.

tamal de quinua tamale made of quinoa-based dough. Cooked quinoa is mixed with lard and seasonings, then stuffed with a piece of pork, wrapped in a banana leaf and steamed.

TASTY **tamalitos verdes** green tamales. Spinach and cilantro color the fresh ground corn dough that is wrapped in cornhusks and steamed. Also called *humitas verdes*. See recipe p. 54, and photo in color insert, fourth page, middle left.

tarta de quinua savory pancakes made with quinoa and egg, layered with a filling of spinach in sour cream. See recipe, p. 63, and photo in color insert, last page, top.

té tea.

té manzanilla chamomile tea.

té puro black tea.

NATIONAL FAVORITE **tiradito** Japanese-influenced type of *ceviche* made with long, fine strips of fish flattened with the blade of a knife. *Tiradito* is always served extremely fresh with a variety of sauces, nearly always including Key lime juice and some type of chile pepper, but lacking the sliced onions typical of Peruvian *ceviche*.

torrejas cinnamon-flavored French toast, often with raisins and almonds.

torrejas de choclo pancakes made with fresh ground corn, eggs, milk and (often), melting cheese.

torrejas de quinua savory pancakes made from cooked quinoa, grated carrot, onion and parsley mixed with eggs and flour.

torta de chocolate chocolate cake.

torta de tres leches "three milk cake." Rich yellow cake soaked in a mixture of evaporated milk, sweetened condensed milk and fresh milk, topped with whipped cream or meringue and fruits. Also called *pastel de tres leches* and *tres leches*.

tortilla de choclo omelet-like pancake made with fresh ground corn.

tortilla de huevo omelet.

tortilla de raya omelet-like pancake made with herbs and pieces of dried stingray. REGIONAL CLASSIC

tostones twice-fried plantains. See *patacones*. REGIONAL CLASSIC

tres leches "three milk cake." See *torta de tres leches*.

trigo atamalado stew made with wheat berries, potatoes, onion, garlic, chile peppers and cheese. It is garnished with olives and slices of hard-boiled egg.

triple colorful triple-decker luncheon sandwich. Fillings include sliced tomatoes, avocado and egg salad, with liberal amounts of mayonnaise holding things together. *Triple* also refers to a platter of three items: fried chunks of pork (*chicharrones de chancho*), a stuffed *rocoto* chile pepper (*rocoto relleno*) and a cold salad of chopped pig's feet, onions, potatoes, parsley and salt (*sar de patita*). A FAVORITE

trucha aponada breaded, fried trout. See color insert for photo, last page, bottom right.

trucha rellena stuffed trout.

tules de encaje lace cookies.

turrón de Doña Pepa three thick yellow slabs of anise-flavored shortbread stuck together with honey or syrup. The top is sprinkled with colorful little candies. NATIONAL FAVORITE

uchucuta condiment made from ground Brazil nuts, cilantro, parsley and chile peppers. Also called *ají picante*.

uchullawa boiled potatoes seasoned with chile peppers and a *huacatay* sauce (*huacatay* is a pungent herb).

yacu chupe chowder made green with fresh herbs, including oregano, mint, *huacatay* (a pungent herb), cilantro and parsley. REGIONAL CLASSIC

Yacu chupe includes potatoes, corn, cheese and eggs. Another name for this dish is *chupe verde*.

yuca a la brasa grilled yuca. This dish is called *rumu kusashqa* in Quechua.

yuca rellena cooked, mashed yuca surrounding spicy ground beef and a slice of hard-boiled egg, then deep fried. The dish is similar to its potato cousin *papa rellena*.

yuquita rellena de mariscos croquettes of mashed, cooked yuca stuffed with a seafood mixture.

zambumbia cocktail made with *pisco* (Peruvian grape brandy), pineapple juice, Key lime juice, crushed crackers, raw sugar syrup, cinnamon and cloves, all poured over crushed ice.

NATIONAL FAVORITE   **zarza** See *salsa criolla*. Also spelled *sarsa*.

zarza de patitas de chancho cold salad of chopped pig's feet, onions, potatoes and parsley. Also called *sar de patita*.

Foods & Flavors Guide

This chapter contains a comprehensive list of foods, spices, kitchen utensils and cooking terminology in Spanish (and in some cases in Quechua, the Inca language), with English translations. In Spanish, **ch** is considered a separate letter, so entries beginning with **ch** appear separately after entries beginning with **c**. Likewise, **ll** and **ñ** alphabetize as separate letters after **l** and **n**, respectively. We have cross referenced certain spelling variations for some words. For example **v** and **b** may be used interchangeably in Spanish. Quechua words are transliterated in many different ways. The hard **k** sound may be spelled with a **c, k, q** or **qu**. If you have difficulty finding a word in this *Guide,* try spelling it phonetically to see the possible alternatives.

The *Foods & Flavors Guide* will be helpful in interpreting menus and for shopping in the lively and fascinating outdoor markets. You will find that prices are indicated on food for sale in the markets, but often the items themselves are not identified. Therefore, if you don't recognize something, why not inquire, "What is this called?" (see *Helpful Phrases,* p. 79). Write down the answer phonetically, and use this *Guide* to help identify it.

a la chorillana in the style of Chorillos, a suburb of Lima that once was a small fishing village. Fish and meat are prepared in a spicy onion and tomato sauce.

a la huancaína in the Huancayo style: in a cold sauce of cheese, evaporated milk, oil, Key lime juice, chile pepper, crushed crackers, onion, garlic, salt and pepper, blended until creamy. See *papas a la huancaína, Menu Guide.*

a la loretana in the style of the department of Loreto: served with palm heart salad, fried plantains and fried yuca.

a la norteña cooked with a lot of cilantro.

a la olla cooked in a clay pot.

a la parrilla grilled.

a la patarashca typically steamed in jungle leaves with false cilantro (*sacha culantro*), onions and garlic.

a la plancha griddle-seared.

a lo macho with a topping of diced shellfish.

aceite oil.

aceite de ajonjolí sesame oil.

aceite de oliva olive oil.

aceituna olive.

aceituna de botija Alfonso olive (*Olea europea*), a large, mild-flavored, dark-purple olive grown in Peru.

aceituna negra black olive.

aceituna verde green olive.

acha fish (*Medialuna ancietae*) inhabiting rocky sections along Peru's Pacific coast. Also called *mero* (*mero chino*).

achira starch-rich tuber grown in the warm valleys of the Andes. It comes from an edible plant (*Canna edulis*) related to the ornamental canna lily, and is one of the oldest foods cultivated in Peru. The sweet, mealy tubers are eaten raw or cooked, and also made into a starch that is used to prepare biscuits and bread. The leaves of the plant have a culinary use as food wrappers around a filling in the manner of tamales or *juanes*. See *juane, Menu Guide*.

aderezo dressing; seasoning; condiment.

adobado marinated and cooked in a garlic, chile pepper and vinegar sauce.

adobo marinade. *Adobo* also refers to dishes made with marinated meats, such as *adobo de chancho*. See *Menu Guide*.

adormidera poppy seed.

agridulce sweet and sour.

agrio sour.

agua water.

agua con hielo ice water (not recommended for travelers unless ice cubes have been made with bottled water). Also called *agua helada*.

agua fría cold water. It may or may not have ice.

agua helada ice water; also called *agua con hielo*.

agua mineral mineral water with (*con*) or without (*sin*) carbonation (*gas*).

aguaje ovoid tropical palm fruit (*Mauritia flexuosa*) about 2–3 inches long and covered with horny brown scales, with a thin layer of yellow-orange flesh that surrounds a single large seed.

aguardiente distilled spirits.

aguardiente de pisco colorless brandy distilled from grapes. See *pisco*.

aguaymanto yellow-orange fruit (*Physalis peruviana*) about ¾-inch in diameter, which is encased in a papery, beige husk. It is eaten raw and made into sauces and preserves. English names for this fruit include cape gooseberry, goldenberry and ground cherry. Also called *cereza del Perú* (cherry of Peru).

ahipa (ajipa) leguminous plant (*Pachyrhizus ahipa*) related to *jícama* that is grown for its crispy, watery, tuber-like roots, which are eaten raw or cooked.

ahumado smoked.

ají chile pepper.

ají amarillo moderately hot, finger-shaped chile pepper (*Capsicum baccatum*), which is 4–6 inches long. Despite its name (literally, yellow chile pepper), it has a deep orange color when ripe. It is the most commonly used pepper in Peru and is grown throughout the country. Seeded peppers are used raw as a garnish, cooked with foods or made into a paste, which colors food a bright yellow besides adding piquancy. Other names for this chile pepper are *ají verde, ají fresco* and *ají escabeche*. When dried it is called *ají cuzqueño, ají mirasol* and *ají amarillo seco*.

ají amarillo seco moderately hot, deep yellowish-red chile pepper, which is the dried version of *ají amarillo*. Other names for the dried *ají amarillo* pepper are *ají cuzqueño* and *ají mirasol*.

ají ayuyu hot, aromatic chile pepper, which grows in the Amazon. It is oval or shaped like a banana pepper, and can be yellow, orange, light purple or green. Also called *ayuyu*.

ají cereza cherry pepper, a hot, round chile pepper (*Capsicum annuum*), which is about ¾-inch in diameter and dark maroon when ripe.

ají colorado hot, finger-shaped chile pepper (*Capsicum chinense*), which is 3–5 inches long and brilliant reddish-purple when ripe. When dried, this pepper becomes burgundy-colored and is called *ají panca*.

ají cuzqueño moderately hot, deep yellowish-red chile pepper, which is the dried version of *ají amarillo*. Other names for the dried *ají amarillo* pepper are *ají amarillo seco* and *ají mirasol*.

ají charapita very hot, tiny (about ¼–½ inch in diameter), round, orange chile pepper (*Capsicum chinense*) grown in the Amazon. Also called *charapita*.

ají dulce bell pepper. Also called *ají pimiento* and *pimientón*.

ají escabeche moderately hot, finger-shaped chile pepper (*Capsicum baccatum* var. *pendulum*), which is 4–6 inches long and has a deep orange color when ripe. Other names for this chile pepper are *ají amarillo, ají verde* and *ají fresco*. See *ají amarillo*.

ají fresco moderately hot, finger-shaped chile pepper (*Capsicum baccatum* var. *pendulum*), which is 4–6 inches long and has a deep orange color when ripe. Other names for this chile pepper are *ají amarillo, ají escabeche* and *ají fresco*. See *ají amarillo*.

ají limo very hot, pendant-shaped chile pepper (*Capsicum frutescens*) about 3 inches long and 1–1½ inches wide, which can be red, yellow, orange, purple or white. It grows primarily near the northern coast of Peru.

ají mirasol moderately hot, deep yellowish-red chile pepper, which is the dried version of *ají amarillo*. Other names for the dried *ají amarillo* pepper are *ají cuzqueño* and *ají amarillo seco*.

ají mochero mild chile pepper used for its flavor. It owes its name to the Moche culture and grows between the valleys of Virú and Jequetepeque on the northern coast of Peru. Peppers are thin, 1–2 inches long and are used unripe (green) or ripe (yellow).

ají mono very hot, slightly curved, finger-shaped chile pepper (*Capsicum baccatum*) about 4–5 inches long and ¾ inch wide, which is red when ripe. It is grown in the jungle and is unlikely to be found outside of local markets.

ají montaña hot, long, finger-shaped chile pepper, which can be red, orange, green or purple.

ají panca hot, burgundy-colored, finger-shaped, dried version of the *ají colorado* chile pepper (*Capsicum chinense*).

ají pinguita de mono very hot, small, pointed chile pepper (*Capsicum annuum*) about ½ inch to 1 inch long, which is red when ripe. This pepper grows in the jungle and is sold in regional markets.

ají rocoto super-hot, medium-size, apple-shaped chile pepper (*Capsicum pubescens*), which is green, yellow or (more typically) red when ripe, and has small black seeds. It grows at high altitude in cooler climates.

ají verde moderately hot, finger-shaped chile pepper (*Capsicum baccatum* var. *pendulum*), which is 4–6 inches long and has a deep orange color when ripe. Other names for this chile pepper are *ají amarillo, ají escabeche* and *ají fresco*. See *ají amarillo*.

ajinomoto monosodium glutamate (MSG).

ajo garlic.

ajonjolí sesame.

al carbón charcoal-grilled.

al gusto to taste.

al horno oven-baked.

al lado on the side.

al mojo de ajo in garlic and butter.

al tiempo room temperature.

al vapor steamed.

albahaca basil.

albaricoque apricot.

alcachofa artichoke.

alcaparra caper.

alcaravea caraway.

algarroba carob, a thorny mesquite tree (*Prosopis pallida*) in the legume family, which grows in warm, dry climates. It is prevalent in the northern coastal deserts of Peru. Its fruit (a pod) is enjoyed fresh for its sweet pulp or is ground into a cocoa-like powder.

aliño seasoning mixture used as a spice rub on meat, poultry or fish. It also is used to flavor soups and stews.

almeja clam.

almendra almond.

almíbar light, sweet syrup.

almuerzo mid-morning meal; lunch.

alubia green bean or string bean. Also called *vainita*.

alubia pallar large white Lima bean or butter bean (*Phaseolus lunatus*) generally sold dried. Also called *pallar*.

alverja green pea; also called *arveja* and *guisante*.

alverjado common name for green bean in the northern coastal area of Peru.

amaranto amaranth, a broad-leaf plant (*Amaranthus caudatus*) with tiny, highly nutritious seeds called *kiwicha*.

amargo bitter.

amarillo yellow.

anana pineapple.

anguila eel; baby eel is *angula*.

anona oval to heart-shaped green fruit (*Annona cherimola*), 4–8 inches long, with a variable surface pattern of either small bumps or indentations resembling thumbprints. The scrumptious white pulp of this tropical beauty is sweet, creamy, and tastes like vanilla custard. Also called *cherimoya*.

anticucho appetizer of marinated tidbits of meat or fish grilled on skewers (*palito de anticucho*) made from a bamboo-like reed.

añuje agouti, a large rodent; see *carne de monte*.

api Quechua word for soup.

apio celery.

arazá round, green or yellow fruit (*Eugenia stipitata*) made into juice, marmalade and ice cream.

árbol del pan breadfruit (*Artocarpus altilis*).

arracacha smooth-skinned root vegetable (*Arracacha xanthorrhiza*) resembling a parsnip or white carrot, native to the Andes. *Arracacha,* also called *zanahoria blanca,* or white carrot, is a relative of carrot and celery. The root's crisp white or yellow flesh, which tastes somewhat like celery, is fried, boiled or baked and eaten in stews and salads. Its stalks are used in salads or eaten as a vegetable.

arroz rice.

arroz moldeado molded rice.

arveja green pea; also called *alverja* and *guisante*.

arvejón chickpea (*Cicer areitinum*). Also called *garbanzo*.

asado roasted or broiled.

FOODS & FLAVORS GUIDE

atún tuna.

avena oats.

aves poultry.

ayuyu hot, aromatic chile pepper, which grows in the Amazon. See *ají ayuyu.*

azafrán saffron.

azúcar sugar.

azúcar rubia brown sugar.

bacalao salted, dried cod.

batán stone or wooden board for grinding grain.

batida blended fruit drink with alcohol. Milk is sometimes included.

batido blended milk drink with fruit and other flavorings; also called *licuado.*

baya berry or any small fruit with seeds or stones.

bebida beverage.

berenjena eggplant.

berro watercress.

betarraga beet; also called *remolacha.*

bien cocido (meat) well done.

bijau jungle plant (*Heliconium* sp.) with a large leaf that becomes flexible and paper-like with heat. It is used to wrap and steam foods such as *juanes.* See *juane, Menu Guide.*

bistec beefsteak.

bizcocho biscuit or cake; a cake is also called *pastel* and *torta.*

blanco white.

bocadillo snack, sandwich.

bocadito appetizer.

bocarone sardine.

bodega winery or wine cellar.

borrego lamb; also called *cordero.*

botella bottle.

brassería eatery serving grilled chicken.

bróculi broccoli.

buñuelo fritter.

cabello de angel "angel's hair" marmalade made with *lacayote* squash fibers.

cabra goat.

cabrito young goat (kid).

cacahuate Spanish word for peanut; the Arawak word *maní* is in more common usage. Also called *inchik* in Quechua.

café coffee, which may be ordered *con crema* (with cream), *con leche* (with milk) or *con azúcar* (with sugar).

caigua (caihua) hollow, mild-flavored, climbing squash (*Cyclanthera pedata*) with a twisted, undulating shape. It has thin, pale-green skin and large, flat black seeds, and is typically served stuffed or in soups. Also spelled *cayhua*.

caimán cayman, an alligator-like repile eaten in the Amazon.

caimito (caymito) light-yellow to green fruit (*Pouteria caimito*) about 4 inches long, with a round to oval shape, smooth skin and sweet, white, very moist plum-like flesh. Until completely ripe, the fruit contains a gummy latex.

calabacita zucchini.

calabaza pumpkin, squash.

calamar squid.

caldo broth.

caliente hot.

callos tripe; also called *guatita, librillo, mondongo* and *tripa*.

camarón freshwater crayfish or shrimp (*Cryphiops caementarius*). A seawater shrimp is called *langostina*.

camote sweet potato. Pale- and purple-skinned varieties are found in Peru. The pale-skinned sweet potato has firm, bright-orange flesh. The purple-skinned sweet potato has pale, starchy flesh and is enjoyed baked. In some regions it is not highly regarded and is used to feed animals.

camu camu small, round fruit (*Myrciaria dubia*) grown on a bush. It is about ¾ inch in diameter with purple-red skin and juicy yellow pulp that is very acidic and rich in vitamin C.

cancha dried yellow popping corn that is fried in a little oil and eaten as a snack. The kernels swell and pop but do not turn inside out. They become crispy and golden-brown, and are enjoyed salted. *Cancha* is especially relished with *ceviche*. Also called *cancha amarilla, cancha chulpe* (*chulpi*) and *maíz para tostada*.

canela cinnamon.

cangrejo crab.

canilla shank (cut of meat).

caña de azúcar sugar cane.

cañán lizard served whole in the area of Virú on the northern coast of Peru.

caqui persimmon.

carachama primitive, mud-burrowing, armored (scaly) catfish (*Acanthicus hystrix*) found in the Amazon River. Its flesh is highly regarded.

carambola star fruit.

carne meat.

carne de cerdo pork; also called *carne de chancho*.

carne de monte meat of jungle animals eaten in the Amazon. Such animals—some of which are endangered—include the land tortoise (*motelo*), tapir (*sacha vaca*), monkey (*mono*), deer (*venado*), peccary (*sajino*), and large rodents such as *paca* (also called *majaz* and *picuro*) and agouti (*añuje*).

carne de res beef.

carne de venado venison.

carne molida ground meat.

carnero mutton.

carrillera jowl.

carrizo bamboo-like reed (*Phragmites ommunis*) used to make skewers for grilling food; see *palito de anticucho*.

carta menu.

castaña chestnut.

castaña de brasil Brazil nut.

cayhua type of squash; see *caigua*.

cazuela two-handled casserole dish. *Cazuela* is also a soup; see *Menu Guide*.

cebada barley.

cebolla onion.

cebolla (cebollita) china scallion.

cebolla roja red onion.

cebollinos chives.

cecina salted, dried meat.

cena supper.

centeno rye.

cerdo pig; pork is *carne de cerdo* or *carne de chancho*.

cereza cherry; also called *guinda*.

cereza del Perú "cherry of Peru," the ground cherry; see *aguaymanto*.

cerveza beer.

cerveza negra dark beer.

cevichería (cebichería) restaurant specializing in *ceviche* (*cebiche*), Peru's national dish of fish or seafood "cooked" in lime juice.

ciruela plum or prune.

clara de huevo egg white.

clavo clove; also called *clavo de olor*.

cocina kitchen.

coco coconut.

cocona oblong to round tropical fruit (*Solanum sessiliflorum*) up to 4 inches long with smooth yellow-orange, red-brown or purple-red skin. The sepals remain attached to the fruit. The flesh is cream-colored except for some yellow pulp in the center.

cochayuyo type of large brown seaweed (*Antarctica durvillaea*) eaten in coastal towns in salads and other dishes.

cojinova fish known as palm ruff (*Seriolella violacea*) used primarily for *ceviche* or for frying. Its flesh has a slightly reddish cast.

col cabbage; also called *repollo*.

col de bruselas Brussels sprouts.

col morada red cabbage.

colado strained.

colador strainer, colander.

colapez unflavored gelatin.

coliflor cauliflower.

comedor dining room.

comida food; midday meal.

comida para llevar take-out food.

comino cumin.

concha bay scallop (*Argopecten purpuratus*).

concha negra strong-tasting black scallop (*Anadara tuberculosa*).

conejo rabbit.

congrio conger eel.

conserva jam; jelly.

copa cup; goblet.

copoasú oblong aromatic fruit pod (*Theobroma grandiflorum*) with pulp that is eaten fresh or made into juices, desserts, ice creams and jams. *Copoasú* is in the same family as cocoa (*cacao*).

corazón heart.

cordero lamb; also called *borrego*.

corvina type of sea bass (*Cilus gilberto*) commonly used to make *ceviche*.

costilla chop; also called *chuleta*.

crema cream.

crema de leche lightly soured cream. Also called *crema fresca*.

criadilla testicle.

criollo dishes that are a fusion between native Indian and foreign influences.

crudo raw.

cubierto table service consisting of a napkin and cutlery, often just a knife and fork.

cuchara tablespoon.

cuchara de madera wooden spoon.

cuchara de medir measuring spoon.

cucharada tablespoonful.

cucharadita teaspoonful.

cucharita teaspoon.

cuchillo knife.

cuello neck.

cuenta bill or check.

culantro cilantro.

cúrcuma turmeric.

curuba banana passion fruit (*Passiflora mollissima*), an oval, yellowish-green fruit about 4 inches long with orange flesh surrounding many little black seeds, which grows on a vine in the mountains. Also called *tumbo*.

cuy guinea pig (*Cavia porcellus*).

chancaca hard, molded, unrefined sugar made by boiling sugar-cane juice until the liquid has evaporated. Also called *panela*.

chancho pork; also called *carne de cerdo* and *carne de chancho*.

charapilla uchu slender, elongated, aromatic, hot red chile pepper grown in the Amazon.

charapita tiny (about ¼–½ inch in diameter), round, very hot, orange chile pepper (*Capsicum chinense*) grown in the Amazon. Also called *ají charapita*.

charqui thin strips of dried meat; jerky.

cherimoya oval to heart-shaped green fruit (*Annona cherimola*), 4–8 inches long, with a variable surface pattern of either small bumps or indentations resembling thumbprints. The scrumptious white pulp of this tropical beauty is sweet and creamy, and tastes like vanilla custard. Also called *anona*.

chico small.

chicha fermented drink made from a variety of grains, fruits and vegetables, most commonly corn (*chicha de jora*).

chicha de año corn drink resembling wine, which is fermented for 1–3 years.

chicha de jora beer-like fermented corn drink of pre-Inca origin, which is prepared as a home brew in the Andes. The finished product has a bubbly froth, and is served at room temperature. Besides its consumption as a social drink, *chicha de jora* is a flavoring agent in many dishes.

chicha morada nonalcoholic drink made with purple corn, pineapple rind and chopped fruit (see recipe, p. 44).

chicharrónes small pieces of deep-fried meat or fish.

chichería place where *chicha de jora,* a traditional fermented beverage made from corn, is produced and served.

chifa restaurant serving Chinese-Peruvian fusion cooking, stir-fried Peruvian food with the addition of some traditional Chinese ingredients. Traditional Chinese dishes also are on the menu.

chifles fried plantain or banana chips.

chinchulies lamb intestines.

chinto small, oval, red chile pepper with a pointed end, grown in the jungle.

chirivía parsnip.

chita marine grunt (*Anisotremus scapularis*), a fish found in temperate waters with rapid currents.

chivo male goat.

choclo fresh, large-kernel, white corn on the cob. Cobs are cut in thick rounds for use in soups and as an accompaniment to many dishes, especially *ceviche*.

chocoteja chocolate-covered *teja,* a variety of traditional, oval-shaped candy made in the department of Ica. See *teja.*

chocho leguminous plant (*Lupinus mutabilis*) grown at high altitude in the Andes. Its protein-rich beans are used in soups, stews and salads, but must first be soaked to remove their bitterness. Also called *tarwi* and *lupin.*

chonta palm heart, obtained from the *huasai* (*huassai*) palm (*Euterpe precatoria*) or *pijuayo,* the peach palm (*Bactris gassipaes*). Also called *palmito.*

chorizo spicy pork sausage.

choro Peruvian ribbed mussel (*Aulacomya ater*) with a silvery black shell.

chuleta chop; cutlet. Also called *costilla.*

chulpe variety of dried corn used to make toasted corn (*cancha*).

chuño blanco white *chuño,* a potato that has been converted into a light-weight, skinless nugget with characteristic hardness and chalky white color using an ancient Andean freeze-drying technique. It keeps for several years without spoiling and is an important part of the diet of the people living in the Andean highlands. *Chuño* is ground into flour or softened in water and cooked in various dishes. It is fare for feasts and special occasions. Also called *moraya* and *tunta.* Compare with *chuño negro.*

chuño negro black *chuño,* small, irregular, bitter potatoes, either whole, in pieces or damaged, freeze-dried using a shorter and somewhat different process from that used for making white *chuño.* The potatoes blacken due to oxidation, turning gray after dehydration. Black *chuño* is part of the everyday diet, not feast fare. See *chuño blanco.*

chupe chowder; savory stew.

churro stick of fluted fried dough rolled in sugar and sometimes filled with sweet milk caramel. Also the name of the moon snail eaten in the Amazon.

chuta large flat bread (about one foot in diameter and two inches thick) made in the village of Oropesa, near Cuzco. When someone is given a stack of three loaves, it signifies that a favor is being asked that cannot be refused.

dátil date.

dehuesado boned.

desayuno breakfast.

doncella large, tiger-striped, shovel-nosed, scaleless Amazon catfish (*Pseudoplatystoma fasciatum*). Also the name for a closely related catfish (*P. tigrinum*) with dramatic, but uniform, vertical stripes.

dorado salmon-like fish (*Salminus maxillosus*), which has a golden-yellow body with lengthwise rows of dots and reddish-orange fins. The fish is found in the Amazon River and can reach over 40 pounds.

dulce sweet.

dulce de leche sweet milk caramel used as a filling or frosting. Also called *manjar blanco*.

durazno peach; also called *melocotón*.

durazno blanquillo white peach, which opens easily.

duro hard.

elote ear of corn.

empanada sweet or savory pastry resembling a turnover.

en su concha in its shell.

endivia (endibia) endive; also called *escarola*.

eneldo dill.

ensalada salad.

entrada first course.

escarola endive; also called *endivia (endibia)*.

espárragos asparagus.

espinaca spinach.

estragón tarragon.

faba broad bean; fava bean. Also called *haba*.

fideo noodle.

flan custard.

fonda small, simple eatery in a marketplace.

frambuesa raspberry.

fresa strawberry.

fresco fresh.

fríjol (fréjol) bean; also called *menestra*.

fríjol canario canary bean (*Phaseolus vulgaaris*), a pale-yellow, oval, smooth-skinned bean native to Peru. Also called *fríjol peruano*.

fríjol de palo variety of lentil (*Dolichos lablab*) with a thin, white scar along its edge where it was attached to the inside of the pod. The lentils are brown, red or beige, and have to be cooked properly because raw seeds are toxic. Also called *lenteja bocona*.

fríjol peruano canary bean (*Phaseolus vulgaaris*). See *fríjol canario*.

frío cold.

fruta fruit.

galleta cookie or biscuit (cracker).

gallina hen.

gamitana fruit- and seed-eating fish (*Colossoma macropomum*) found in the Amazon River, which is equipped with powerful, molar-like teeth adapted for crushing its food. Its oval-shaped body has an olive-green back and a black underside. These colors meet unevenly at the midline, producing a pronounced jagged pattern. *Gamitana* reach lengths of three feet and weights of 60 pounds and are prized for their delicious flesh. Also called *pacu*.

ganso goose.

garbanzo chickpea; also called *arvejón*.

gorgoño black grape grown in the Amazon and used to make wine.

grageas colored candy sprinkles.

granada pomegranate.

granadilla variety of passion fruit (*Passiflora ligularis*) about the size of a lemon with sweet and juicy, whitish-yellow pulp surrounding many small seeds. The pulp primarily is eaten fresh or made into drinks.

grasa fat; grease.

guaba ice cream bean, a legume (*Inga feuillei*) with huge (up to 2 feet long), boomerang-shaped pods and large seeds, which are surrounded by sweet white pulp eaten fresh as a prized fruit snack. Also spelled *huaba* and called *pacae* (*pacay*).

guanábana soursop (*Annona muricata*), an asymmetrically heart-shaped, green fruit up to a foot long with skin bearing many soft short projections.

guatita tripe; also called *callos, librillo, mondongo* and *tripa*.

guayaba guava (*Psidium guajava*).

guinda cherry; also called *cereza*.

guindón prune.

guisante green pea; also called *alverja* and *arveja*.

guiso stew.

haba broad bean; fava (*faba*) bean.

harina flour.

helado ice cream.

hielo ice.

hierba herb.

hierba luisa lemon grass.

hierba salvia sage.

hierbabuena mint; also spelled *yerbabuena*. Another name for mint is *menta*.

hígado liver.

higo fig.

hinojo fennel.

hoja leaf.

hoja de bijau large leaf of the heliconium plant, used to wrap foods for steaming.

hoja de laurel bay leaf.

hoja de milpa cornhusk; also called *panca* (*panca de concha*).

hongo mushroom.

horno oven.

huaba ice cream bean, a legume (*Inga feuillei*) with huge (up to 2 feet long), boomerang-shaped pods and large seeds, which are surrounded by sweet white pulp eaten fresh as a prized fruit snack. Also spelled *guaba* and called *pacae* (*pacay*).

huacatay strong-flavored herb (*Tagetes minuta*) in the marigold family used fresh as a seasoning. The dark-green leaves are long and thin, and have jagged edges. English names include black mint and Peruvian black marigold.

huachinango red snapper; also called *pargo*.

huerto small orchard or fruit garden.

huevo egg. An egg can be cooked *duro* (hard-boiled), *escalfado* (poached), *estrellado* (sunny side up), *estrellado volteado* (over easy), *frito* (fried), *revuelto* (scrambled) and *tibio* (soft-boiled).

huminta (humita) pre-colonial antecedent of the tamale made with ground fresh corn or half-cooked corn, and a variety of additional ingredients such as squash. The mixture, which can be sweet or savory, is wrapped in cornhusks and boiled or steamed. The Spanish gave these corn-filled *humintas* the Spanish name of *tamales*.

Inca Kola national soft drink of Peru, a cloying, yellow soda that tastes like bubble gum.

inchik peanut in Quechua. Peruvians typically refer to the peanut with the Arawak word *maní*. The Spanish *cacahuate* is less commonly used.

inguiri boiled plantain, a popular food in the jungle.

jalea jelly. *Jalea* also is a dish of deep-fried seafood, potatoes and yuca.

jamón ham.

jamón del país country ham.

jarabe syrup.

jarabe de algarrobina sweet syrup made from ground, dried pods of the carob tree, *algarroba*.

jarabe de goma sugar syrup.

jengibre (jenjibre) ginger; also called *kión*.

jícama light-brown tuber (*Pachyrhizus erosus*) with crispy, white flesh, which is sweet when fresh. It typically is eaten raw.

jora sprouted corn; see *maíz jora*.

juane jungle version of the tamale, a traditional dish of the Amazon. See *Menu Guide*.

jugo juice; also called *zumo*.

jugo de carne juices from cooked meat; consommé.

kañiwa broad-leaf plant (*Chenopodium pallidicaule*) that grows at high altitude in the Andes and produces a small (about 1 mm), nutritious grain, which is toasted and ground into flour for use in soups and breads. The grain is also used to make beverages served hot or cold. Also spelled *qañiwa*.

karachi small fish (*Orestia sp.*) native to Lake Titicaca, which is highly prized in the city of Puno. It typically is eaten with *chuño,* potatoes that have been freeze-dried. See *chuño blanco* and *chuño negro,* this *Guide*.

King Kong large rectangular (about 4 × 6 inches and 2 inches thick) or round (about 4 inches in diameter) pastry with thick layers of fillings between cookie-like crusts. The filling is *manjar blanco* (sweet milk caramel) with bits of dried fruit. Some versions have additional layers such as quince jelly, pineapple and figs. These hefty treats are wrapped in cellophane and sold on the street in Chiclayo and Trujillo. *King Kong* pastries in both cities are similar, but those in Chiclayo have harder cookie crusts.

kión ginger; also called *jengibre (jenjibre)*.

kiwicha amaranth, a broad-leafed plant (*Amaranthus caudatus*) grown at high altitude in the Andes. Its small, nutritious grain, also known as

FOODS & FLAVORS GUIDE

amaranto, is ground into flour for baked foods. Popped grains or flakes made from whole, rolled grains are eaten as breakfast cereals. Leaves and stems from young plants are boiled and eaten as a vegetable.

lacayote sweet, oval-shaped squash (*Cucurbita ficifolia*) weighing up to 24 pounds, with white flesh and black or white seeds. The skin is green or white and can be spotted or striped. *Lacayote* is eaten boiled or made into preserves and puddings. The seeds are baked and eaten as a snack. Also called *zambo.*

langosta lobster.

langostina seawater shrimp.

leche milk.

leche condensada condensed milk.

leche evaporada evaporated milk.

lechón suckling pig. A three-week old suckling pig is called *mamoncito.*

lechuga lettuce.

lechuga redonda iceberg lettuce.

lechuga romana Romaine lettuce.

legumbre vegetable.

lengua tongue.

lenguado sole; flounder.

lenteja lentil.

lenteja bocona variety of lentil (*Dolichos lablab*). See *fríjol de palo.*

levadura yeast.

librillo tripe; also called *callos, guatita, mondongo* and *tripa.*

licuado blended milk drink with fruit and other flavorings. Also called *batido.*

licuadora blender.

lima lime. See also *limón,* this *Guide.*

lima con pupo light-yellow or light-green lime with a nubbin on one end. The fruit is sweet with a slightly spicy flavor.

limón small, round, juicy Key lime (*Citrus aurantifolia*). It is used to "cook" raw fish in the very popular dish called *ceviche* (*cebiche*). The Key lime is also called *limón agria* and *limón sutil.*

lisa mullet.

loche type of knobby squash (*Cucurbita moschata*) about a foot long with seedless, yellow-orange flesh and dark-green skin. Also called *zapallo loche.*

lomo tenderloin or filet mignon.

lúcuma much-appreciated, nutritious, green-skinned native fruit (*Pouteria lucuma*) about 3 inches in diameter with firm, starchy, yellow-orange flesh and one or more large brown seeds. It is eaten raw. Dried, ground *lúcuma* is used to flavor ice cream, puddings, beverages, cakes and cookies.

luisa lemon grass.

lupin leguminous plant (*Lupinus mutabilis*) grown at high altitude in the Andes. Its protein-rich beans are used in soups, stews and salads, but must first be soaked to remove their bitterness. Also called *chocho* and *tarwi*.

llonque unrefined alcohol made from sugar cane. Also spelled *yonque*.

maca plant (*Lepidium meyenii*) grown at high altitudes in the central Andes. Its sweet and spicy, radish-like tubers are packed with nutrients and touted as fertility- and libido-enhancers. The tubers, which may be purple, yellow, or yellow with purple bands, are eaten fresh or made into beverages, puddings, jams and flour. The cress-like leaves of the plant are eaten in salads or fed to guinea pigs, an important meat source in the Andes.

macambo large, oval, yellowish-brown fruit (*Theobroma bicolor*) with woody, longitudinal ribs interconnected by similarly woody strands that form an irregular meshwork on the surface. The creamy yellow flesh of the *macambo* is eaten fresh or made into juice or ice cream. The white seeds, which taste like fava beans, are skewered with pampas grass stalks and roasted. *Macambo* is in the same family as *cacao* and *copoasú.*

macha razor clam.

machacado shredded, crushed, puréed.

machica toasted barley flour. Also called *harina de cebada tostada.*

maduro ripe; mature.

maicena cornstarch.

maíz dried corn, as opposed to fresh corn.

maíz jora sprouted, sun-dried corn that is crushed and used to make *chicha de jora,* a fermented beverage brewed in the Andes, dating back to pre-Inca cultures. Also called *jora.*

maíz morado purple corn native to the Andes. *Maíz morado* is used to prepare *chicha morada,* a fruity, nonalcoholic drink (see recipe, p. 44), and *mazamorra morada,* a fruit pudding (see *Menu Guide*).

maíz mote dried kernels from a variety of corn (*choclo*) with large white kernels. Also called *mote.*

maíz para tostada popping corn; see *cancha.*

majaz fruit-eating giant rodent (*Agouti paca*) eaten in the Amazon. Also called *paca* and *picuro.* See *carne de monte.*

malagueta small, very thin, hot red chile pepper.

mamey a grapefruit-size fruit (*Mammea americana*) with light-brown, dull, leathery skin and fibrous orange flesh surrounding 1–4 large, brown seeds.

mamoncito three-week old suckling pig; see *lechón*.

mandarina tangerine.

maní peanut in the Arawak language (most common usage). Peanut is also called *cacahuate* (in Spanish) and *inchik* (in Quechua).

manjar blanco sweet milk caramel used as a filling or frosting. Also called *dulce de leche*.

manteca shortening, lard.

mantequilla butter.

manzana apple.

manzanilla chamomile, used for tea.

maracuyá vine-grown, purple or yellow oval passion fruit (*Passiflora edulis*) about the size of a lemon, which is somewhat wrinkled when ripe. Its yellow pulp is enjoyed fresh or made into beverages and preserves.

mariscos seafood.

marisquería seafood restaurant.

marraqueta roll with crispy crust and soft interior, which is made without fat.

masa dough.

mashua plant (*Tropaeolum tuberosum*) grown at high altitudes in the Andes for its small, nutritious roots. There are several varieties, distinguished by their root shape and color. Common root colors are white, yellow, red, or purple. Roots are cooked to reduce their sharp, peppery taste, and are enjoyed in stews and soups.

mauka plant (*Mirabilis expansa*) grown in the Andes for its edible but slightly bitter, protein-rich tubers and succulent stems. The astringency of the roots can be reduced by exposure to the sun. The white- or yellow-colored roots typically are eaten in stews and soups.

mayonesa mayonnaise.

medio half.

medio hecho (meat) medium rare.

mejorana marjoram.

melaza molasses.

melocotón peach; also called *durazno*.

melloco Andean plant (*Ullucus tuberosus*). See *olluco*.

membrillo quince.

menestra bean; also called *fríjol*.

menta mint; also called *hierbabuena* (*yerbabuena*).

menta verde spearmint.

merluza hake.

mermelada jam.

mero (mero chino) fish (*Medialuna ancietae*) inhabiting rocky sections along Peru's Pacific coast. Also called *acha*.

mero murique broomtail grouper (*Mycteroperca xenarcha*), a large fish primarily inhabiting deep waters off the coast of northern Peru. Its flesh is rosy and transparent.

miel (miel de abeja) honey.

migas bread crumbs.

mijo millet.

mococho type of seaweed eaten in coastal towns.

molde de carne meat loaf.

molido ground.

molle pink pepper-like berry from the Peruvian pepper tree (*Schinus molle*), which is used as a spice.

mollete muffin.

mondongo tripe; also called *callos, guatita, librillo* and *tripa*.

mono monkey; see *carne de monte*.

montado with fried egg on top.

mora blackberry.

moraya potato freeze-dried using an ancient technique. See *chuño blanco*.

morcilla blood sausage.

mortiño blueberry of the Andes (*Vaccinium floribundum*), a small (about ¼ inch in diameter), round, bluish-black berry with many tiny seeds.

mostaza mustard.

mote dried kernels from a variety of corn (*choclo*) with broad, flat, white kernels. Also called *maíz mote*.

motelito tiny, round, orange or white chile pepper, which grows in the jungle.

motelo land tortoise; see *carne de monte*.

nabo turnip; daikon radish.

naranja orange.

naranjilla orange-yellow fruit (*Solanum quitoense*) with green pulp and many small seeds. It is related to the tomato and grown in the foothills of the Andes. *Naranjilla* is used primarily to make juice.

nata agria sour cream.

níspero del japón yellow loquat (*Eriobotrya japonica*), a pear-shaped fruit with up to five seeds. It tastes somewhat like a sour cherry.

níspero del monte small brown fruit (*Bellucia grossularioides*) with aromatic, acidic juice and many tiny seeds.

novoandino new Andean, a term referring to the cooking style that is a fusion of native, pre-colonial ingredients and techniques with elements of nouvelle cuisine.

nuez nut.

nuez encarcelada pecan.

nuez moscada nutmeg.

nuña type of hard-shelled bean (*Phaseolus vulgaris*) grown in the Andes at high altitude. Unlike most beans, which must be boiled before eating (a difficult task at high altitudes), this bean bursts out of its seed coat when heated in a little oil. The popped beans are enjoyed as a snack or side dish.

ñuto cookie made with yuca flour and flavored with *aguardiente,* an alcoholic beverage made from sugar cane.

oca plant (*Oxalis tuberosa*) grown at high altitude in the Andes. Its brightly colored (white, yellow, pink, red, purple, yellow or black), shiny tubers have crisp white flesh ranging in taste from sweet to tangy, depending on the variety. *Oca* tubers can be sweetened by leaving them in the sun for six to seven days. Sweet ones can be eaten raw, but most are cooked and added to stews and soups, baked, or candied like sweet potatoes.

olla traditional Peruvian earthenware cooking pot.

olluco plant (*Ullucus tuberosus*) with colorful tubers—white, yellow, pale-green, pink, orange or purple—resembling potatoes, which is grown at high altitude in the Andes. The firm and crispy yellow flesh of the tubers is covered with skin thin enough to require no peeling before eating. Tubers are enjoyed boiled or used to thicken soups and stews. Julienned *olluco* is sold in the markets, packed in plastic bags. Also called *melloco* and spelled *ulluco.*

ostra oyster.

paca fruit-eating giant rodent (*Agouti paca*) eaten in the jungle. Also called *majaz* and *picuro*. See *carne de monte.*

pacae (pacay) ice cream bean, a legume (*Inga feuillei*) with huge (up to 2 feet long), boomerang-shaped pods and large seeds, which are surrounded by sweet white pulp eaten fresh as a prized fruit snack. Another name for this legume is *guaba* (*huaba*).

pacu Amazon fish (*Colossoma macropomum*). See *gamitana.*

paiche one of the largest scaled fish in the Amazon River basin (*Arapaima gigas*). Specimens average over 6 feet long, making this one of the most important and prized food fish. Its smooth white flesh typically is salted and dried (*paiche seco*). *Paiche seco* fillets, sold in markets rolled up like jellyrolls, require overnight soaking to remove the salt before cooking.

palabrita small, strong-tasting surf clam (*Donax marincovichi*) inhabiting the intertidal zone of sandy, coastal beaches in southern Peru. These small clams are enjoyed in soups and stews.

palillo saffron of the Andes, a tasteless food colorant ground from the dried, yellow-orange roots of a native herb (*Escobedia grandiflora*). It is also called *raiz de color*, or "coloring root." Dried, ground turmeric is substituted for *palillo* and even sold as *palillo*.

palito de anticucho skewer made from *carrizo*, a bamboo-like reed (*Phragmites ommunis*), and used to grill small tidbits of marinated fish or meat (*anticuchos*) for appetizers.

palmito palm heart. See *chonta*.

palometa round-bodied Amazon River fish (*Mylossama aureum*) with a layer of fat under the skin. The flesh of this fish in the piranha family is prized.

palta avocado.

pallar large white lima bean or butter bean (*Phaseolus lunatus*), generally sold dried. Also called *alubia pallar*.

pan bread.

pan de tres puntas dinner roll specialty of Arequipa with three slight bumps on top, created by making two evenly spaced slashes on the roll before it is baked. The bumps represent the three mountains surrounding the city.

panca (panca de concha) cornhusk; also called *hoja de milpa*.

pancito roll.

panela hard, molded, unrefined sugar made by boiling sugar-cane juice until the liquid has evaporated. See *chancaca*.

pango (pangu) term used in the Amazon for food cooked without spices or additions other than salt.

papa potato.

papa amarilla yellow potato; also called *papa criolla*.

papa huayro bumpy, hard-to-peel potato with tender, whitish-yellow flesh and purple skin.

papa morada purple potato.

papa seca type of preserved potato. To make *papa seca,* bitter varieties of potatoes are cooked, peeled, cut into small bits and dried in the sun until hard. The dried bits are reconstituted in water before use in dishes such as the classic *carapulcra* (see *Menu Guide*).

papaya arequipeña small papaya (*Carica cundamarcensis*) that grows in Arequipa, which is used to make juice.

pargo red snapper; also called *huachinango*.

parinari oblong jungle fruit (*Couepia* spp.), 1–1½ inches long, which is reddish brown when ripe. The soft, creamy pulp tastes somewhat like an apple.

pasa raisin.

pasta de ajos garlic paste.

pastel cake; also called *bizcocho* and *torta*.

pato duck.

pavo turkey.

pechuga breast.

pejerrey the Peruvian silverside, a small, smelt-like fish (*Odontesthes regia*) about 5 inches long with pinkish flesh and a silvery stripe on the side. It lives near the shore along the Pacific coast. A freshwater variety is larger.

pellejo de chancho soft pork skin with some associated fat.

pepián soft "pudding" made with ground fresh corn, chile-pepper paste and seasonings. Ground rice or roasted peanuts may be substituted for the corn.

pepino (pepinillo) cucumber. See also *pepino dulce*.

pepino dulce sweet cucumber melon, a fruit (*Solanum muricatum*) with refreshing, watery flesh, which comes in several shapes, sizes and colors. The one commonly seen in the markets is the size of a goose egg and has smooth yellow skin with purple stripes and pale-yellow flesh. Typically, the rind is not eaten. Small seeds are clustered in the center of the fruit. The fruit maintains its Spanish name in English usage and in both languages is often shortened simply to *pepino*.

pera pear.

perejil parsley.

perro caliente hot dog.

pescado fish; also called *pez*.

pescado salado dried, salted fish.

pez fish; also called *pescado*.

pez espada swordfish.

picada minced.

picante spicy.

picantería traditionally an eatery serving typical Peruvian foods, family style, cooked in clay pots over a wood fire. Homemade *chicha de jora,* corn beer, always accompanies the food. Ample amounts of chile peppers make many of the dishes hot (*picante*), thus the name *picantería*. They are particularly well established in Arequipa, a city in the southern highlands known for its spicy foods.

picuro fruit-eating giant rodent (*Agouti paca*) eaten in the jungle. Also called *paca* and *majaz*. See *carne de monte*.

pierna thigh and drumstick.

pierna de cordero leg of lamb.

pijuayo peach palm tree (*Bactris gassipaes*) native to the Amazon. It bears ovoid fruit, also called *pijuayo,* which are about 1–2 inches long with yellow-red, orange, or even green skin when ripe. In the markets, clusters of the fruit can be found still attached to the stems. The trees are an important source of palm hearts (*chonta, palmito*), which typically are cut in thin ribbons and enjoyed in salads.

pimienta blanca white pepper.

pimienta negra black pepper.

pimientón bell pepper. Also called *ají dulce.*

piña pineapple. Some varieties have reddish rinds.

pipa coconut water.

piqueo finger food; appetizer.

pisco (aguardiente de pisco) colorless brandy distilled from grapes grown in the Ica valley. The grapevines were brought by the Spaniards, who named the brandy for the port of Pisco, from which it was shipped. *Acholado* is a type of *pisco* distilled from a blend of different grape varieties; *aromático* is made with Italia, Moscatel, Muscat or Torontel grapes; *mosto verde* is distilled from grapes that have not been fully fermented; and *puro* is distilled from the black Quebranta grape.

pituca taro, a starchy tropical tuber (*Colocasia esculenta*) with somewhat hairy brown skin and white or pale purple flesh.

plátano banana.

plátano macho plantain.

plato plate. *Plato* also refers to a menu item (dish).

plato de fondo main dish.

poco hecho cooked rare.

polvo de hornear baking powder.

pollo chicken.

pollería eatery specializing in rotisserie chicken.

pomelo round to pear-shaped citrus fruit (*Citrus maxima*) considered the ancestor of the grapefruit. *Pomelo,* the largest member of the citrus family, is less tasty than true grapefruit and has a thicker rind.

poro leek.

postre dessert.

pota giant squid. The flesh is cut into long, ¼-inch strips, giving the appearance of a plate of thick noodles when served.

pucunu uchu short, dull-skinned, finger-shaped, yellowish-orange hot chile pepper with an irregular surface. *Pucunu uchu* grows in the jungle.

pulpo octopus.

qañiwa Andean grain. See *kañiwa*.

queso cheese.

queso andino *queso fresco* made in the Andes. *Queso andino* has more fat than *queso fresco* and takes longer to prepare. A special pattern of cross hatching on the outside identifies the cheese as from the Andes. It is not a melting cheese.

queso de cabra goat cheese.

queso fresco firmly packed, lightly salted, fresh white cheese, which takes about a week to prepare. It is not a melting cheese.

quimbombó (quingombó) okra.

quinta eatery serving regional foods and featuring beer.

quinua quinoa, a hardy, broad-leaf plant (*Chenopodium quinoa*) that grows in the Andes. It produces a flat, pale-yellow grain that has a pointed, oval shape resembling sesame seeds. Varieties producing grain that is white, pink, orange, red or black can also be found. The protein-rich grain is ground into flour for baked foods and eaten whole in soups. Breakfast cereals are made from whole grain that is popped or rolled into flakes. After quinoa is cooked it becomes translucent and the external germ on its surface forms an opaque, incomplete ring twisted outward. Before cooking, the grain has to be washed to remove a bitter, natural detergent (saponin) in its coating. Quinoa grains are high in iron, an essential nutrient that is even more important for blood oxygen capacity at high altitudes.The leaves are eaten raw in salads or as a leafy vegetable, like spinach.

rábano radish.

rábano picante horseradish.

raiz de color saffron of the Andes, a tasteless food colorant. See *palillo*.

raya ray; skate.

refresco cold, non-alcoholic drink.

remolacha beet; also called *betarraga*.

repollo cabbage; also called *col*.

revuelto mixed or stirred; scrambled.

riñón kidney.

robalo snook (*Centropomus undecimalis*), a fish related to the sea bass.

rocoto super-hot, medium-size, apple-shaped chile pepper (*Capsicum pubescens*), which is green, yellow or (more typically) red, when ripe, and has small black seeds. It grows at high altitude in cooler climates and traditionally is served stuffed (*rocoto relleno*); see *Menu Guide*. Also called *ají rocoto*.

romero rosemary.

rumu Quechua word for yuca, a tuber rich in starch.

sábalo Amazon River fish (*Brycon erythropterum*) with red-tinged fins.

sacha culantro false cilantro (*Eryngium foetidum*), an aromatic herb used in the jungle. The leaves, about 3 inches long and 1½ inches wide, are much larger than true cilantro and have a more pungent cilantro-like flavor. Also called *siuca culantro*.

sacha maní false peanut (*Leonia* sp.), a dark, round, flattish, oil-rich seed from the fruit of a climbing plant that grows in the jungle. It is eaten toasted.

sacha papa false potato (*Dioscorea trifida*), a large, dark-skinned root that grows in the Amazon and is eaten cooked. It resembles an elongated sweet potato and has starchy purple flesh that dissolves easily in the mouth.

sacha tomate false tomato or tree tomato, an egg-shaped fruit (*Cyphomandra betacea*) that grows on a small tree native to the Andes. The fruit has shiny reddish-purple skin with flesh that resembles a tomato but has a piquant flavor. The fruit is eaten raw or cooked and is made into sweet or savory dishes. Also called *tomate de árbol* and *tamarillo*.

sacha vaca tapir; see *carne de monte*.

sajino peccary; see *carne de monte*.

sal salt.

salchicha hot dog; sausage.

salmón salmon.

salsa sauce.

salsa de carne gravy.

saltado stir-fried dish such as *lomo saltado* (see *Menu Guide*) that includes crispy fried potato strips (French fries).

sandía watermelon.

sauco Andean elderberry (*Sambucus peruviana*).

seco dry; also refers to a stewed preparation with a thick sauce.

servilleta napkin.

sesos brains.

sidra cider.

sillau soy sauce.

siquisapa Quechua word for "big-ass ant," the giant, flying queen of the leaf-cutter ants of the Amazon. Its large abdomen is eaten fried.

siuca culantro false cilantro (*Eryngium foetidum*). See *sacha culantro*.

sofrito seasoning mixture with garlic, onions, tomatoes, bell peppers and herbs.

sopa soup.

suave soft; smooth.

sudado food steamed aromatically with seasonings and chile peppers without the addition of liquid. The ingredients give off sufficient moisture to allow the food to steam cook. See recipe for *pescado sudado*, p. 55.

suri fatty larvae of the palm weevil (*Rhynchophorus palmarum*), which feed off the trunks of certain felled palm trees. They are much appreciated in the jungle where they are eaten fried.

Sybarita commercial mixture of powdered *ají panca* chile pepper, turmeric and other spices, which is used to flavor and color foods.

tallarin spaghetti.

tamal tamale; Spanish name for *humintas* (*humitas*), the Quechua word for a preparation of grated or ground fresh corn or half-cooked corn, and a variety of additional ingredients, wrapped in cornhusks and boiled or steamed. Modern corn packets contain fresh corn, hominy or corn flour, in addition to Old World ingredients such as lard, chicken or pork, olives and chopped hard-boiled eggs. Banana leaves can also be used as a wrapper.

tamarillo egg-shaped fruit (*Cyphomandra betacea*). See *sacha tomate*.

t'anta wawa bread baby, typically an oval, flat bread with a tiny painted face on it, which is made for special occasions. For example, it is placed on the graves of relatives on All Souls' Day early in November. *Wawa* is the Quechua word for the sound babies make when they cry.

taperiba yellow mombin (*Spondius mombin*), a small, oval, yellow or green fruit about 1½ inches long and 1 inch wide. The flesh is yellow, translucent, tart and juicy.

tarwi leguminous plant (*Lupinus mutabilis*) grown at high altitude in the Andes. Its protein-rich beans are used in soups, stews and salads, but must first be soaked to remove their bitterness. Also called *chocho* and *lupin*.

taza cup.

té tea.

teja traditional oval-shaped candy made in the department of Ica. It is filled with sweet milk caramel (*manjar blanco*), nuts and candied fruit, and coated with fondant or melted chocolate. The candy is wrapped in paper, which is twisted at the top with the ends sometimes cut to create a festive fringe.

tenedor fork.

ternera veal.

tetera teapot.

tibio warm. *Huevos tibios* are soft-boiled eggs.

tiburón shark.

tierno tender.

tirabuzón corkscrew.

tocino bacon.

tollo shark-like fish (*Mustelus abbotti*) used salted and dried, or fresh. Also spelled *toyo*.

tomate tomato.

tomate de árbol tree tomato (*Cyphomandra betacea*). See *sacha tomate*.

tomatillo acidic, tomato-like fruit (*Physalis philadelphica*) covered with a papery husk, which is removed before cooking. *Tomatillo* is used while still green.

tomillo thyme.

toronja grapefruit.

torreja fritter; French toast.

torta cake; also called *bizcocho* and *pastel*.

tortilla omelet.

tortuga turtle.

tostada toast; toasted.

toyo shark-like fish (*Mustelus abbotti*) used salted and dried, or fresh. Also spelled *tollo*.

tramboyo blenny (*Labrisomus* sp.), a small, warm-water marine fish that lives along reefs and in holes.

trigo wheat.

tripa tripe; also called *callos, guatita, librillo* and *mondongo*.

trucha trout.

tucunaré peacock bass (*Cichla ocellaris*), a beautifully colored fish with a silvery body and a brown back. Behind the eye is a characteristic mottled patch of black spots. It also has three vertical dark blotches along the midline and a black and yellow "eye" spot on the tail fin. *Tucunaré* is a prized food fish in the Amazon.

tumbo (tumbo serrano) banana passion fruit (*Passiflora mollissima*), an oval, light yellowish-green fruit about 4 inches long with orange flesh surrounding many little black seeds. The fruit, which grows on a vine in the mountains, is acidic and appears to have been used to "cook"or preserve fish before citrus fruits were introduced into Peru by the Spaniards. Also called *curuba*.

tumbo gigante giant, vine-growing passion fruit (*Passiflora quadrangularis*), an aromatic, oval, pale yellowish-green fruit up to 12 inches long and 6 inches wide, which grows better in more tropical parts of Peru. The edible outer layer of flesh is melon-like, white or pink and watery, and the core is filled with many small seeds surrounded by sweet white pulp. The flesh of *tumbo gigante* tastes blander than that of *tumbo*.

tuna fruit of the prickly pear cactus (*Opuntia ficus-indica*).

tunta potato freeze-dried using an ancient technique. See *chuño blanco*.

turi ridged gourd (*Luffa acutangula*), which reaches lengths of two feet and bears ten longitudinal ridges and a tapered neck. Young gourds are sliced and cooked as a vegetable.

uchu Quechua word for chile pepper.

ulluco Andean plant (*Ullucus tuberosus*). See *olluco*.

uva grape.

vainita green bean or string bean. Also called *alubia*.

vasija bowl.

vaso drinking glass.

vegetal vegetable.

venado deer; see *carne de monte*.

vinagre vinegar.

vinagre de chincha vinegar made from *chicha de jora*.

volteados suaves (eggs) over easy.

yacón plant (*Polymnia (Smallanthus) sonchifolia*) with brown-skinned tubers having white, yellow, orange or purple flesh. The tubers are eaten raw like an apple, boiled or baked. Because they are naturally sweetened by sugars not metabolized by the human body, the tubers are ideal food for diabetics and dieters.

yema de huevo egg yolk.

yerbabuena mint; also spelled *hierbabuena*. Another name for mint is *menta*.

yonque unrefined alcohol made from sugar cane. Also spelled *llonque*.

yuyo cloud ears; small, dried fungus used in traditional Chinese cooking and in Chinese-Peruvian dishes served at Chinese restaurants (*chifas*).

zambo sweet, oval-shaped squash (*Cucurbita ficifolia*). See *lacayote*.

zanahoria carrot.

zanahoria blanca "white carrot." See *arracacha*.

zapallito italiano zucchini.

zapallo super-sized, round squash (*Curcurbita moschata*) with dark green or mottled dark green skin and brilliant yellow-orange flesh. Specimens can weigh up to 30 pounds. *Zapallo* typically is sold by the slice in markets.

zapallo loche type of knobby squash (*Cucurbita moschata*) about a foot long with seedless, yellow-orange flesh and dark-green skin. Also called *loche*.

zapote round to ovoid fruit (*Pouteria sapota*) with dark-brown, leathery skin and orange to deep-red flesh. The fruit has up to four large, brown seeds and can grow to 9 inches long and weigh up to 5 pounds.

zumo juice; also called *jugo*.

Restaurants

Chefs at These Eateries Taught Us Much about Peruvian Food

A Puerta Cerrada, Av. Bolognesi 752, Barranco, <u>Lima</u>, Tel: (01) 477-0686, http://www.restaurantapuertacerrada.com, chef Luis Felipe Arizola Gadea.

Astrid y Gastón Restaurant, Cantuarias 175, Miraflores, <u>Lima</u>, Tel: (01) 444-1496, ayg@qnet.com.pe.

Casa-Hacienda San José, Km. 9, Carretera a El Carmen, <u>Chincha</u>, Telefax: (56) 22-1458, hsanjose@terra.com.pe, http://www.haciendasanjose.com.pe

Club Colonial, Grau 272, Plaza de Armas, Huanchaco, <u>Trujillo</u>, Tel: (44) 46-1015, ccolonial@yahoo.com, chef/owner Anne Debert de Kesch.

El Catador Restaurant and Winery, Fundo Tres Esquinas, Subjanjalla, <u>Ica</u>, Tel: (56) 40-3295.

El Dorado Plaza Hotel, Napo 258, <u>Iquitos</u>, Tel: (94) 22-2555, chef Diego Garcia Vela.

El Huerto de mi Amada, <u>Azpitia</u>, department of Lima, Tel: (01) 98862031, chef Blanca Arias de Caycho.

El Mochica, Jr. Bolivar 462, <u>Trujillo</u>, Tel: (44) 22-4247.

El Rincón del Pato, Av. Leguia 270, <u>Lambayeque</u>, Tel: (74) 28-2751.

El Señorío de Sulco, Malecón Cisneros 1470, Miraflores, <u>Lima</u>, Tel: (01) 441-0183, http://www.senoriodesulco.com, chef Flavio Solórzano Alvarez.

El Tiradito, Av. Aviación 4628, Surquillo, <u>Lima</u>, chef/owner Fidel Trigozo.

Fiesta Restaurante Gourmet, Av. Salaverry 1820, <u>Chiclayo</u>, Tel: (74) 20-1970, fiestagourmet@terra.com.pe.

Hotel Paracas, Av. Paracas 173, <u>Paracas</u>, Tel: (56) 54-5100, hparacas@terra.com.pe, http://www.hotelparacas.com, chef Guillermo de la Fuente Sattui.

Huaca Pucllana, General Borgoño Cuadra 8 S/N, Miraflores, <u>Lima</u>, Tel: (01) 445-4042, chef Marilú Madueño.

Huanchaco Beach, Malecón Larco 602, Huanchaco, <u>Trujillo</u>, Tel: (44) 46-1484, huanchacobeach@hotmail.com, chef/owner Maria de Lam.

Inkafé, Sonesta Posadas del Inca, Plaza Manco II 123, <u>Yucay</u>, Tel: (84) 20-1107, http://www.sonesta.com.

La Bombonniere, Burgos 415, San Isidro, <u>Lima</u>, Tel: (01) 421-2447, chef Jorge (Coque) Luis Ossio Guiulfo.

La Lucila Picantería, Grau 147, Sachaca, <u>Arequipa</u>, Tel: (54) 28-3596.

La Patarashca, Jr. Lamas 261, <u>Tarapoto</u>, Tel: (42) 52-3899, César Reátegui y Elia García, chefs/owners.

La Perla de las Flores, Calle La Florida 998, <u>Chiclayo</u>, Tel: (74) 23-2520, perladelasflores@latinmail.com, chef Gloria Yaipen Chafloque.

Machu Picchu Pueblo Hotel, Av. Ferrocarril S/N, <u>Machu Picchu Pueblo Village</u>, Tel: (84) 21-1122, central@inkaterra.com, http://www.inkaterra.com.

Machu Picchu Sanctuary Lodge, Hiram Bingham Ave. (at the entrance to the Machu Picchu Inca Citadel ruins), <u>Machu Picchu</u>, Tel: (84) 21-1038 and 21-1039, chef Michael Raas.

Manos Morenos, Av. Pedro de Osma 409, Barranco, <u>Lima</u>, Telefax: (01) 467-0421.

Map Café, Plaza de las Nazarenas 231, <u>Cuzco</u>, Tel: (84) 24-2476, mapcafe@amauta.rcp.net.pe, chef Hernán Castañeda.

Ñaylamp, Av. 2 de Mayo 239, Barranco, <u>Lima</u>, Tel: (01) 467-5011, chef Santiago Solari Morgan.

Punta Sal, Av. Conquistadores 948, San Isidro, <u>Lima</u>, Tel: (01) 441-7431, puntasal@terra.com.pe, http://www.puntasal.com, chef Adolfo M. Perret Bermúdez.

Quinta el Eulalia, Choquechaca 384, <u>Cuzco</u>, Tel: (84) 24-1380, chef Felicidad (Adela) Tapia Alvarez.

Restaurante del Hotel Paracas, Av. Paracas 173, <u>Paracas</u>, Tel: (56) 54-5100, http://www.hotelparacas.com, chef Guillerimo de la Fuente Sattui.

Sol de Mayo, Jerusalén 207, Yanahuara, <u>Arequipa</u>, Tel: (54) 25-4148, chef Alcario Callyahua.

Sonesta Posadas del Inca, Pancho Fierro 194, San Isidro, <u>Lima</u>, Tel: (01) 221-2121, http://www.sonesta.com, chef Rafael Piqueras.

Sonesta Posadas del Inca, Plaza Manco II, Yucay 123, <u>Yucay</u>, Tel: (84) 20-1107, epasquel@sonestaperu.com, http://www.sonesta.com, chef Eduardo Pasquel.

Tunupa, Km. 77, Carretera Pisac-Ollantaytambo, <u>Valle Sacrado</u>, Tel: (84) 63-0206, chef/owner Antonia Cossio Arana.

Tunapa, Portal Confituria 233, Plaza de Armas, <u>Cuzco</u>, Tel: (84) 25-2936/23-1281, chef/owner Antonia Cossio Arana.

Wa Lok, 864-878 Jiron Paruro, Barrio Chino, <u>Lima</u>, Tel: (01) 427-2656.

Bibliography

Anonymous. *Comidas Tipicas del Peru por Departamentos*. Lima, Peru: Editora Lima SA, 1988.

Bawden, Garth. *The Moche*. Cambridge, Massachusetts: Blackwell Publishers, 1996.

Blanchard, Peter. *Slavery & Abolition in Early Republican Peru*. Wilmington, Delaware: Scholarly Resources, Inc., 1992.

Bowser, Frederick P. *The African Slave in Colonial Peru: 1524–1650*. Palo Alto, California: Stanford University Press, 1974.

Bray, Tamara L., editor. *The Archaeology and Politics of Food and Feasting in Early States and Empires*. New York: Kluwer Academic / Plenum Publishers, 2003.

Brenuil, compiler. *Peruvian Dishes. Traditional Dishes Simplified*. Lima, Peru: Librerías ABC S.A., 2002.

Bushnell, G.H.S. *Peru: Ancient Peoples and Places,* revised edition. New York: Frederick A. Praeger Publishers, 1969.

Cabieses, Fernando. *Cien Siglos de Pan,* 2nd edition. Lima, Peru: Universidad San Martín de Porres, 1996.

Charney, Paul. *Indian Society in the Valley of Lima, Peru, 1532–1824*. Lanham, Maryland: University Press of America, Inc., 2001.

Cisneros, Antonio, Alejandro Ferreyros, Luis Jochámovitz, María Rostworowski, Raúl Vargas, Javier Wong and Walter H. Wust. *Cebiches del Perú*. Lima, Peru: Gráfica Biblos, 2004.

Coe, Sophie D. *America's First Cuisines*. Austin, Texas: University of Texas Press, 1994.

Crosby, Alfred W., Jr. *The Columbian Exchange: Biological and Cultural Consequences of 1492*. Westport, Connecticut: Greenwood Press, 1972.

Custer, Tony. *The Art of Peruvian Cuisine*. Lima, Peru: Quebecor World Perú, 2003.

Davies, Nigel. *The Ancient Kingdoms of Peru*. London: Penguin Books, 1997.

Egg, Antonio Brack. *Frutas del Perú*. Lima, Peru: Universidad San Martín de Porres, 2003.

Haas, Jonathan, Shelia Pozorski and Thomas Pozorski, editors. *Origins and Development of the Andean State*. Cambridge, England: Cambridge University Press, 1987.

Hastorf, Christine A. Cultural implications of crop introductions in Andean prehistory. In *The Prehistory of Food: Appetites for Change,* edited by Chris Gosden and Jon Hather, pp. 35–58. London: Routledge, 1999.

Hemming, John. *Monuments of the Incas.* Boston, Massachusetts: Little, Brown and Company, 1982.

Hinostroza Clausen de Molina, Gloria. *Cocinas Regionales Peruanas - 2: Centro del Perú.* Lima, Peru: Universidad San Martín de Porres, 1999.

Keatinge, Richard W., editor. *Peruvian Prehistory: An Overview of Pre-Inca and Inca Society.* Cambridge, England: Cambridge University Press, 1992.

Kijac, Maria Baez. *The South American Table: The Flavor and Soul of Authentic Home Cooking from Patagonia to Rio de Janeiro, with 450 Recipes.* Boston, Massachusetts: The Harvard Common Press, 2003.

Lathrap, Donald W. *The Upper Amazon.* New York: Praeger Publishers, 1970.

Lockhart, James Marvin. *Spanish Peru, 1532–1560: A Portrait of Peruvian Colonial Society at Its Origin.* PhD thesis, University of Wisconsin–Madison, 1967.

Moseley, Michael E. *The Incas and Their Ancestors: The Archaeology of Peru,* revised edition. London: Thames & Hudson, Inc., 2001.

National Research Council. *Lost Crops of the Incas: Little-known Plants of the Andes with Promise for Worldwide Cultivation.* Report of an ad hoc panel of the Advisory Committee on Technology Innovation, Board on Science and Technology for International Development. Washington, DC: National Academy Press, 1989.

Pillsbury, Joanne, editor. *Moche Art and Archaeology in Ancient Peru.* Washington, DC: National Gallery of Art, 2001

Rice, Prudence M. The Spanish Colonial Wineries of Moquegua, Peru. In *Historical Archaeology, Journal of the Society for Historical Archaeology,* Volume 23, Number 2, pp. 41–49, 1989.

Rick, John W. *Prehistoric Hunters of the High Andes.* New York: Academic Press, 1980.

Roosevelt, Anna, editor. *Amazonian Indians from Prehistory to the Present: Anthropological Perspectives.* Tucson, Arizona: The University of Arizona Press, 1994.

Ruiz, Casilda Naar. *Cocinas Regionales Peruanas - 1: Amazonía.* Lima, Peru: Universidad San Martín de Porres, 1999.

Stewart, Watt. *Chinese Bondage in Peru: A History of the Chinese Coolie in Peru, 1849–1874.* Durham, North Carolina: Duke University Press, 1951.

Super, John C. and Thomas C. Wright. *Food, Politics, and Society in Latin America.* Lincoln, Nebraska: University of Nebraska Press, 1985.

Wust, Walter H. *Guía de Especies Útiles de la Flora y la Fauna Silvestres.* Lima, Peru: Santuarios Naturales del Perú, 2003.

Wust, Walter H., editor. *Comer & Viajar en el Perú.* Lima, Peru: El Comercio, 2004.

Index

INDEX

ORDER FORM

Please send me:

_____ copies of **Eat Smart in Peru** - $13.95

_____ copies of **Eat Smart in India** - $13.95

_____ copies of **Eat Smart in Turkey (2nd Edition)** - $13.95

_____ copies of **Eat Smart in Brazil (2nd Edition)** - $13.95

_____ copies of **Eat Smart in Indonesia** - $12.95

_____ copies of **Eat Smart in Mexico** - $12.95

_____ copies of **Eat Smart in Morocco** - $12.95

_____ copies of **Eat Smart in Poland** - $12.95

Add $2.50 postage (media mail) for one book, $1.00 for each additional book. Wisconsin residents add 5% sales tax. For international orders, please inquire about postal charges.

Check enclosed for $ _____

Please charge my: VISA_____   MASTERCARD_____

Card # _____ Exp. _____

Signature: _____

Name: _____

Address: _____

City: _____ State: _____ Zip: _____

Mail this form to: **Ginkgo Press, Inc.**
2018 Chamberlain Ave., Madison, Wisconsin 53726

Tel: 888-280-7060 • Fax: 608-233-0053
www.ginkgopress.com • info@ginkgopress.com

design   Ekeby
cover design   Susan P. Chwae
color separations   United Graphics, Inc.
printing   United Graphics, Inc.

typefaces   Garamond Simoncini and Helvetica Black
paper   60# Offset